Mandy

BORN DIFFERENTLY. BORN TO SURVIVE

To Tracey & The Ship Staff

"Much Love"

Mandy Martin x

x x x

MANDY MASTERS

Mandy - Born Differently. Born to Survive
Copyright © Mandy Masters 2019

ISBN 978-1-912009-46-6
First published 2019 by Compass-publishing

Edited and typeset by The Book Refinery Ltd
www.thebookrefinery.com

The right of Mandy Masters to be identified as the author of this
work has been asserted in accordance with the Copyright, Designs
and Patents Act, 1988.

This book is a true story.

A CIP catalogue record for this book is available from the
British Library.

Printed and bound by CMP Group - Poole, Dorset.

I'm dedicating my book to my dear mum (Mumsi), who sadly passed away on 21st January 2017. The hearts of everyone in my family were broken, especially mine.

My mother was the strongest and bravest lady that walked this earth. She made me who I am today. My heart will never be mended and my pain will never go away, but I hold very special, treasured memories of her and feel so proud to have been brought up as a normal child in a different way.
I'm so glad that when I finished my book in 2014, my parents read my rough copy. It was just in time, as my dear mum got the beginnings of dementia not long after that.

Until now, my book has been in my drawer waiting to come to life. Mumsi, you were not just my mum, you were my teacher, my life and my world.

You made me the strong woman I am today.
With love and kisses all the way to heaven, your surviving daughter, Mandy xxx

Contents

Foreword

I first met Mandy when I was with my mum Margaret and sister Julie. I was roughly 10 years old. Julie and Mandy were best friends at a lovely special school for children with different disabilities. My sister explained that Mandy was a thalidomide victim and unfortunately was born without arms. One evening, Mandy and her sister Jane were invited to our house for tea (Mandy was about 13). This is the first time I saw Mandy use her feet – she was amazing! From day one, I knew Mandy and I would become close friends. She was so inspiring. I was fascinated that such a beautiful young girl could do everything that I could, and nothing or no one could tell Mandy she couldn't. I soon realised that Mandy was just one of the girls.

Mandy's mother, June, never treated Mandy any differently to the rest of the family; she still had to do her share of the chores to help out. She amazed me the first time I saw her sit on the floor, put a Hoover under her chin and vacuum her room. I'm so proud to have watched Mandy grow from a young teenager to the beautiful, amazing woman she is today. She's a wonderful stepsister and best friend and is someone I can always turn to. Mandy has never let anyone or anything beat her. If anyone said, "Mandy, you can't do…" Whatever it may be, they would have to step aside and watch her. I mean, she's written this book!

I remember going out to clubs, etc., with Mandy and Jane. Mandy used to do our eyebrows, change our hairstyles, pick our clothes out and even do our make up so we looked older than we were – and all this with her tootsies!

I've seen Mandy run a majorette troupe, become a cake maker (creating the most beautiful crinoline doll cakes) and beautician, drive her first car, get married to Wayne, have two beautiful children, eight grandsons, read tarot cards and become a spirit connector.

So, world, all I can say is, "Step back and watch this caring, courageous, amazing lady called Mandy in action." The popular phrase "This girl can" pretty much sums her up. Who wouldn't want to call this inspiring woman their friend? I'm even prouder to call her one of my family.

Sandra Archer

Editor's Note

by Danielle Wrate

I had the pleasure of meeting Mandy several years ago when I was a writer at *Take a Break Fate & Fortune*. My colleagues and I were visiting her home for a reading, and she picked us up from the station in her specially adapted car. I remember being hugely impressed by her driving skills. Mandy is such a confident lady and has such a strong presence that her disability is not something you actually focus on much when you meet her, but now, all this time on, I feel honoured to have read her story and learn more about her struggles and triumphs. What she has overcome is not to be underestimated and her 'can do' attitude, which she developed with the help of her loving and supportive family, is hugely inspirational. Mandy hasn't had it easy yet she hasn't let that stand in her way or stop her from living a full, action-packed life. Even as I type this now, I think of Mandy tapping away on the keyboard with her toes. Next time someone tells me they want to write a book, *but* (insert typical excuse here), I'll be sure to tell them about Mandy. And next time I find myself thinking, "I can't" (let's face it, we all do it from time to time), I'll think of Mandy too.

Introduction

I must admit that talking and typing about my life has produced mixed emotions of happiness and sadness. It's also made me realise that my journey to where I am right now hasn't always been easy.

My story is about how I grew up without arms due to the drug thalidomide. Back in 1961, when I was born, doctors told my parents they should go home without me and get on with living a normal life with their other children. They also said I probably wouldn't make it to my twentieth birthday and would basically be a cabbage. If the doctors had had their way, I wouldn't be writing this now. Luckily, my parents didn't listen to them. Instead, they encouraged me to use my little toes as if they were fingers and treated me no different to my five siblings. Whenever I found something difficult and said, "I can't do this", Mum would reply, "Never say you can't, Mandy." Boy, how her words have stuck strong with me throughout my life's journeys. I've had my ups and my downs and I've laughed and I've cried. You will also be surprised about what I got up to in my teenage years! Throughout, I have always stood strong on my path and conquered many things to be a 'normal' child and adult. I always wanted a husband to love me and to have children with, and I've managed to achieve those dreams.

Many of you must be wondering how I can do things with no arms and no hands. Well, my tootsies did become my fingers and they are very flexible as a result. Nothing was gonna stand in my way. In fact, I think I can do many things better than people with hands.

I never ever wanted to say I was struggling, so to help me cope when I was feeling sad or down I built a seabed deep down in my tummy.

My Seabed

Well, from what I can remember, I was around 11 years old when I imagined I had a seabed deep down in my tummy. When certain things upset me, such as noticing being stared at or overhearing someone saying, "Look, she's got no arms!" I would let that go deep into my tummy, where it would sink in the soft sand. I never wanted to let things get to me and I didn't want my mind to be stressed or to become emotional. Plus, I certainly didn't want my parents to know I was hurting. So, once I had let them sink they were gone. When I started typing my book, I felt my seabed stirring and things coming back. One time, writing about the death of my dear horse, the tears came rolling down my face. I realised that this was therapy for me, as that seabed wasn't meant to stay with me forever. It would clear once I started my life's journey and became who I am today. This happened in around 2014. I knew that I had achieved many things in life and that my seabed was no longer needed.

I'm no longer the little girl from Essex with no arms, I'm me, Mandy Masters, an Earth Angel to many, and an author. But boy did writing about the past unsettle my seabed. I'm glad it did, though, as I now feel free and there isn't a seabed within my belly anymore.

I hope my life's story so far has intrigued you, and will continue to do so as you read about me, Mandy Hornsby, and then me, Mandy Masters. But that isn't all, my friends, as there's another story in my life. Once my daughters got into their teens I went on another pathway and embarked on a special journey. You see, I knew from an early age that I was different, but not because I was born without arms. Oh no, my friends, this was a journey with the spirit world. As early as six years old, I started hearing voices. They would reassure me and repeat, "You are safe, as we are here with you." Wow, was I scared – and I didn't tell a soul. Then, when I was 14 years old, I went to Lourdes in France, where my spiritual connections became even stronger. But I won't go into detail with you all now as my second book will be called, *An Earth Angel's Journey (Mandy on the Road)*.

Those of you who know me as Mandy Masters will have probably read my three-page column in a well-known monthly magazine called *Take a Break Fate & Fortune*, which I have been writing since 2005. I started out with one column and now produce three very interesting pages every month. You may have also come to one of my shows, which I've performed in this country and overseas. You will know all about my spiritual work and how much my wonderful gift has grown on this special pathway. It's probably kept you intrigued and keen to find out what I am doing now and why so many people call me their 'Earth Angel'. Well, my friends, stay tuned for the next chapter in my life. You will be amazed how I have changed the minds of so many sceptical people regarding the existence of life up above in heaven.

Until next time, my good friends. XXX

CHAPTER ONE

The Beginning

On the 20th September 1961, my mother gave birth to me – yep, a baby girl with a difference. I can recall her telling me that throughout her pregnancy she kept saying to her mother that there was something wrong with her baby. Something felt different to when she was pregnant with my three brothers and my sister. Her mother just said she was being daft. I asked Mum what it was she was feeling and she said she felt she was carrying a Down syndrome baby. Another strange thing is that she got a pram before I was born. As the old saying goes, "Never have a pram in your home before your baby's born." It's funny that my mother did just that before my arrival. My mum wasn't superstitious, but it's rather ironic considering what happened next.

When Mum went into labour, my father, who I might say was a real grafter, was at work. He received a call saying I had been born, but there was a problem. When he asked what it was, he was told, "Your daughter has a deformity." My father then asked how my mum was and how she had taken the news. The doctor replied that my mum didn't know, as they had taken the baby away. OMG, my father was appalled and rushed straight to the hospital.

Upon his arrival, a doctor met him, who told him they would take me in to see Mum. But my dad replied, "You can't just take her in without telling my wife there's something wrong first." So my dad had to break the news to my mum, but she already knew something wasn't right. They brought me into the room and uncovered me, and all I know is that they both loved me no matter what was wrong with me. The doctors said to my parents that they didn't have to keep me, leaving them free to go home to their other children and lead a normal life. My parents were having none of it. They said that they were going to take me home and that's just what they did. And this is where my life begins.

Now, you might not know what thalidomide is, so let me explain. It's a drug that was brought out in the '60s for pregnant women who either suffered from sickness or, like my mother, couldn't sleep. No one knew how dangerous this drug was going to be for expectant mothers. There were babies born without arms and legs and with internal damage, too. Not having any arms wasn't easy, but my parents brought me up to use my toes as hands. Seeing others with no limbs made me feel very sad, but I must say that many of them, like me, had a strong determination to live a normal life, and boy did we work hard. Some children were taken from birth and brought up in children's homes, as I guess some parents couldn't accept their defects, which also made me very sad, as I was brought up in a very loving and caring home.

I asked my parents what happened when they took me home and whether they told my siblings about me first. My father said he sat them down and told them they had a little sister who was a bit special. Of course, they wanted to know more and he said that although I was a healthy little girl, my arms were missing. When the day to bring me home arrived, my siblings were waiting for me in the living room. My mother laid me on the floor and uncovered me for them to see. I can remember hearing how one of my siblings said they wanted to see my body, as they had never seen anyone with no arms before, but once they had all had a good look they went off to play and from that day on I was just their little sister and they didn't treat me any different to anyone else in the family. My parents also told me that when I was born they received nasty letters from anonymous people saying I should have been killed at birth. How sad for my parents to have had to read such awful words.

My parents were told that I probably wouldn't survive and may only reach 19. They also said I wouldn't be able to do much and would basically be a cabbage who would never have children. OMG, how wrong were these so-called doctors. I've always said to my parents that if I had hands, I would stick two fingers up and say, "Up yours!" to them. I've done it all, and more.

My parents treated me no different. I was about six months old when my mother heard me rustling a newspaper at the bottom of my pram with my feet. From that day on she encouraged me to use them. She said she used to get her plastic rollers and put them on my toes. Apparently, I loved them! Mum gave me other things to try and grasp with my feet too.

At nine months old, I started standing on my own two feet. Again, the doctors had told my parents I probably wouldn't walk until I was about two, as having no arms would make it difficult for me to balance. But once again I proved them wrong, as I started walking much earlier. Looking at the picture of me taken by *The Sunday Times* back then (there was a lot of media interest in children like me), well, what a strong, determined little person I was. Seeing my big smile made me realise that I was one happy and contented baby. Yep, nothing was going to stop me or get in my way. Standing strong on my chubby legs and with amazing balance, it was clear how ready I was to challenge this world.

When I was about two, Mum took me to a hospital in Roehampton, London, where I was to try a pair of artificial arms. But my parents weren't sure if these would be more of a burden to me and stop me from using my feet. So, as time went on, my mother encouraged me to do more for myself. I can always remember not wanting to pull my knickers up. I would go to the toilet and shout down "Finished!" very loudly. But on one particular day after I'd shouted this, I heard my mother reply, "Pull your knickers up yourself, Mandy!" Well, me being stubborn, I said, "No, I don't want to." My mother replied, "Stay there, then!" Well, at the time I thought she was a horrible mum. It wasn't until I was older that she told me how that used to make her cry, but she knew she had to be hard if I was going to be independent in life. I thank both my parents for doing this, even though at the time I thought they were cruel.

After coming home with the artificial arms, Mum promptly let me out to play with my brothers and sisters. (And yes, I say sisters now as my mother had convinced herself she wouldn't be able to have another normal baby and the doctor's advice was to conceive again to prove that she could. She took this advice and that's where my baby sister comes in.) I went out onto the big playing field at the back of our garden and my mother, who was watching, noticed that the other children were scared of my arms and didn't want to play with me. Mum realised they only knew me without arms and that having these plastic things on my shoulders made me not 'me' somehow. So I didn't end up wearing them.

CHAPTER TWO

My Childhood

I can remember my first day at school. I wasn't aware that my mother had been determined for me to attend a mainstream one or that some of the local ones had said no. Well, my mother was not giving in and made an appointment to talk to the headmistress of Woodside School, Mrs MacAnalley, who allowed me to attend. I can remember lunchtime vividly, as I was placed on a low window shelf to eat my dinner, while the other children ate at tables. This must have affected me as my elder sister Susan started coming to see me at lunchtimes, and we ate our dinner together in the classroom. This went on until I went up to the juniors, when my father came up with a fantastic idea. He knew how much I wanted to eat at a dinner table with my friends, so he got a friend of his at work to help out. More on this later…

Meanwhile, it helps for you to know that on my right shoulder I have the beginnings of an arm, which looks more like a finger. We call this 'my stump'. Had it developed, it would have been an arm. I have a small elbow joint and at the end there's little markings where I guess fingers would have grown. On my left side I have nothing apart from a tiny hole. I must say, as a little girl I loved my right-side stump and found it useful to carry things. I will always remember my youngest brother Kevin letting me slap him around his face when we play fought, and boy could I give a mean little slap. I can also remember my other siblings – Bill the eldest, then Robert, Susan and, finally, my youngest sister, Jane – saying to me, "Come on, Mandy, show us your little muscle." I used to get my little stump out and bend it like you would your arm.

Once I remember going into Grays, our local town, and playing up in Woolworths. I had seen a doll I wanted, which Mum said I couldn't have. Well, I started kicking and screaming, so Mum slapped my leg. A fellow shopper, a lady, could see I had no arms as Mum used to tuck my coat sleeves in (which I must add I hated). She came over and said to Mum, "You wicked woman." My mum replied, "Mandy's no different to my other children and I'm not having her kicking and screaming because she wants a doll." Mum said the lady tutted and walked away.

Anyway, back to the dinner problem. My dad got his friend to weld a metal ring round a fork and a spoon. He then slipped the ring over my stump and OMG I could sit at the table like everyone else and eat. No one will ever really know the feeling that gave me – to think I could sit at a normal table and use my special fork and spoon without needing my feet. My parents don't know just how much that meant to me. When the day came for me to take these two very important items to school, my friends all wanted to carry them and couldn't wait to put them on my stump at lunchtime. From day one, my best friend at infant school was Shirley Hammond. She was a very special friend to me and was like a little mother who was always on hand to get anything I needed. I thought it was only fair that she should crown my little stump. OMG, I was so excited and that day I couldn't wait to get my new utensils onto my stump. I can remember us queuing to get our lunch. Shirley was carrying my fork and spoon and when we finally got our food and went to our table, my heart was beating fast with excitement. When Shirley put the fork and spoon on my tiny little stump, I felt I was normal and just like the others sitting with my feet still in my shoes. I was so proud of my dad for coming up with this genius idea. Thank you, Daddy.

CHAPTER THREE

Family Life

Well, I will start by first introducing you to my parents. Meet my father, Len Hornsby, and my mother, June Hornsby. My parents met when they were very young. My mum was 13 years old and my dad was 18. My mum said she used to stand on the farm gate at the end of the garden of her parents' bungalow in Essex and watch Dad go by – he used to work on the farm.

My mum said my dad was very popular with the girls as he was a very good-looking young man and a Jack the Lad too. They started dating and quickly fell in love. My mum got pregnant two weeks before her 16th birthday and in those days it wasn't good to be pregnant outside of marriage. My mum had a massive falling out with her parents and went to find my dad at the local café where he used to hang out with his friends. She told him that she had run away from home. Together they went down to Grays Beach where they slept in a bus shelter. Mum said it started to snow so my dad took his coat off and covered my mum up. How sweet and romantic was that! The next morning, my dad found this old, empty caravan in the fields, which he warmed with an old oil heater that he managed to get working. Now, you're going to laugh when I tell you this. In the morning when they woke up, they both had very black faces! With the caravan accommodation clearly not working, Dad took Mum to her auntie Maud's home, where she stayed until she had their first child, my brother Billy, who was born in Dec. Later, my parents got on a bus to Grays Register Office and got married on 21st March 1953. In 2013, they celebrated their diamond wedding anniversary. My dad was a very hard worker and loved working on the farm as a young lad. As time went on, he left the farm and worked at Bison's making concrete panels. What a romantic story. I love both my parents dearly.

After Billy, Robert was born, then Susan, Kevin and me. Finally, my baby sister Jane arrived. Let me tell you a little about my memories of my family. Well, I can remember being closer to Susan, Kevin and Jane than I was with Bill and Robert, who were that much older. I have to let you into a little secret about having a bottle until I was about six years old. If ever we had visitors, I would get hold of the bottle's teat in my toes and sling it behind our settee, as I didn't want anyone to know that I still had a bottle. I asked my mum once why I had a bottle for so long and she said that when I used to stay at Roehampton hospital, I always felt unsettled and asked for it, so I guess it was a comfort thing. Bill soon got fed up of having to make tea for my bottle, as I loved a bottle of tea, so one particular evening, which I can remember as if it were yesterday, he put salt around the teat instead of sugar. My dad told him off and I can remember Bill saying, "I hate that manky old teat." After that, Bill didn't make me tea anymore, thank God!

Now, I can remember that Robert didn't like it if people stared at me. I guess he was protecting my feelings. When I started to become aware that I had no arms, I began to feel a bit self-conscious, too. I was about 10 when I went to a family wedding. I remember sitting in the hall behind a table and there was this girl just staring at me, even to the point of coming right up to me. The next thing I remember is Robert telling her off and ordering her to go away. I don't think Robert knew I heard him. I guess the little girl had never seen anyone like me before and was simply curious.

Another memory is of me and Kevin having play fights. As I've mentioned, he would stand in front of me and say, "Come on, then, give us a slap." And, oh boy, out came my stump, which I used to whack Kevin straight round the face.

My memory of my elder sister Susan involves a time when I had to have a few tests done at Roehampton. As I got older, I really started to hate going there. Even now, just thinking about having to stay at that hospital, in the Leon Gillis Ward, makes me get a horrible feeling deep down inside. Anyway, I was playing up and refusing to stay for a week in that awful place, so my mum asked the hospital if Susan could stay with me, and they said yes. Well, once I knew Susan was coming with me I was fine. On the way to Roehampton in the car, I would see Cleopatra's Needle by the River Thames, and the Golden Eagle statue along the Embankment. Then, when we got near Buckingham Palace, I'd spot a statue of horses and a chariot on the left-hand side. That's when I would start to cry, as I knew where I was going. "I'm not staying there!" I would scream. I hated that journey. Then we would get into the hospital and go straight to the café. Again, I can see the café even now as I'm typing this. On the right was a long counter with fresh coffee brewing and lots of yummy cakes and food. On the left and down the middle were tables and chairs arranged in booths. I wanted to stay in the café as long as possible, as I knew I was going to be left. I will always remember the long walk down the corridor. It seemed to go on forever. Then we'd turn down this shorter corridor and on the right were the dreaded entrance and that awful sign, above two doors, which read 'Leon Gillis Unit'. I'm cringing even as I type. The worst bit came next, as we came to two swinging plastic doors. I hated them, as it was here it really hit me that I was in this awful, awful place. However, when Susan came with me, at least I knew it wasn't going to be as bad – yay! When Susan was shown to her bedroom, I couldn't believe she wasn't going to be staying on the ward. I do remember those times I was left on my own. When I was much younger, my mum used to stay with me, but as I got older it was not always easy for her to do this. Dad would be working and there were five other siblings to look after, so Mum had to leave me there by myself at times.

There were many times I had to stay by myself, and I always knew what was coming when we got to the ward and this little nurse with dwarfism called Murphy came over and said, "Come on, Mandy, let's go into the TV room and see what's on," Well, I knew Mum and Dad were planning to sneak out at this point and oh did I cry. Murphy used to sit me on her little lap, bounce me up and down and say, "Mum and Dad will be back soon." It's so strange how remembering little things like that can still give me an upset feeling. In the ward, I remember the beds and cots. The cots were horrible – in my eyes they were big tall monsters and the sides were tall and brown and resembled prison walls. After being shown to my bed, I remember Mum unpacking my clothes and putting them in my locker. Oh, the dreaded locker and the little doors at the top where my toothbrush and paste would go with my brand new flannel, my soap and my towel. I hated hearing the clicking of the locker doors. My mum would do me a chart with squares drawn on the paper and the days written inside them, so every day I could cross a square off and know how many days I would have left until I could go home. Anyway, on the occasion Susan came with me, I thought I'd be sharing a bedroom with her, but the powers that be said it wasn't allowed. This made me very sad. Another horrible memory of bedtime was when the nurse would take me to this bathroom where there was a big, deep bath. There were also these tiny toilets with curtains that you could draw around you. I hated being bathed by the nurses. Afterwards, they would put me on a table and powder me. I despised every minute of it. Then I was tucked up in bed and they would put these blue, dimmed lights on and tell us all to go to sleep. I used to cry so much. I can remember seeing the nurses in the office and there was a TV room where the parents who stayed with their children could go. I hated hearing the *10 O'Clock News* and the 10 dings of Big Ben, as I pictured all my family at home watching it. I could cry now just typing this, as if it were yesterday. So, when it was time to go to bed and, knowing my sister was just down the corridor in her room, I decided to start playing up. I cried and refused to go to bed. The sister in charge told me off. I hated this particular nurse and when she went back to her cosy office, I crept out of bed and snuggled in with Susan. Boy did we get told off in the morning, but I really didn't care because I felt safe with my sister.

Well, I was to have a little blood test done. I had never experienced a needle before and when they said they were going to prick my stump with this little pin, well, no way was I having that done! I ran off, with Susan running after me. When she caught up with me, she reassured me that it was only a little pin prick in order to get a little bit of my blood, so I agreed, but only as long as Susan could hold me. I watched every move the medical professionals made. I remember them tearing a little packet open and seeing a little thing inside that had a sharp looking blade. Thinking back, it was only a tiny pin, but when they got hold of my little stump and picked the object up, I screamed. And yes, I thought I was dying in pain. It's silly thinking about it now, though. So that's my childhood memory of Susan. One very sad memory is that my dear sister is now in heaven and won't know that I've written my book. She died, quite suddenly, on the 20th January, 2010, from a bleed on the brain. In my second book, which I am determined to write, you will learn more about her. Love you forever, sis.

Now to Jane, my younger sister. Well, what can I say? She was always a tough little girl. Thinking back to Christmas time, we always got excited and shared a big double bed together. For one particular year, we wanted a doll in a pushchair. I also wanted an oven that baked cakes. Well, Christmas morning arrived and yes, we were awake very early. We had all these toys at the bottom of our bed and were so pleased Father Christmas had been. I wanted to make cakes and put them in this oven, which was only operated by a battery! There I was making Jane and me these awful-tasting cakes and believing they were really cooking in this light-up oven. I can laugh about it now. Then we wanted to walk round to my Aunty Joan and Uncle Fred's house, to show them our babies in their pushchairs. Well, moving this little pushchair was a bit hard for me, and I can remember pushing it with my belly and it going all over the place, but we got there in the end and I loved it.

My parents treated me no different and I was to be just like my brothers and sisters, although I was a daddy's girl and if ever any of them hit me I would always say, "I'm telling Daddy!" They hated this and would tease me by repeating my words. I can laugh about it now, but they said it was annoying, as even when we were play fighting, if I was losing and not getting my way, I would still threaten to tell all to Daddy when he got home. I loved sitting on his lap when he got home from a long day at work. As soon as he sunk down into the chair, I was on his lap with him. My brothers and sisters used to call me Daddy's Girl and say, "Go on, go tell Daddy." My mum made me do lots of things for myself and now I'm glad, because if it wasn't for both of my parents being strong, I wouldn't be who I am today. My mum said there was one afternoon when she could hear me arguing with my friend. We were at the front of the house and had been playing. We started fighting and my dad called my mum and said, "Get her in." My mum replied, "No, let her fight her battles." One thing I can say is that I was never bullied. I must admit it was probably because I had a bossy streak in me, and a big mouth.

It was at this age when I started imagining my seabed.

I guess my seabed came into my mind and life around about when I was 11. I was now at a new school, where some of the children had never met me. Many stared and asked, "Where are your arms?" I then felt anger and wanted to go back to wearing my false arms again. So, my parents took me back to Roehampton to be re-fitted with them. At my infant and junior schools, all the children knew me, so really I was in my comfort zone. To be honest, the arms were never comfortable. I felt like a bloody robot, but going to the big school with my arms on meant I didn't have to sit on a stall and put my feet up to write. And at least having the arms on meant I could sit on a normal chair like everyone else with a pen in my hand and my feet enclosed in socks and shoes. WOW, I was now the same as everyone else.

When playing with friends, I always wanted to be in charge and to mimic the teacher. My dad made me a playhouse out of concrete panels and put a roof on it, along with windows and a door. The windows only had plastic on them and they ripped as time went on. I will always remember that when gathering in the playhouse in the winter, my friends would hang old blankets over the windows so we didn't get cold. We played mums and dads and I made many mud pies – it was great playing in my playhouse. My friends never treated me any different. To them I was just Mandy. For example, even though Toni Wilson, Tracey Tyson and Joan Bennett were at a different school to me, when we got home, we would usually play together. (Even if I did have to be in charge most of the time! lol.) One thing though, if one of them couldn't come out and it was just three of us well, what's that saying...? "Two's company and three's a crowd." Definitely true with us as we were always having a fallout. That happened one day with me and Joan and we did have a fight, lol, but the following day we still all played together, once again the best of friends, treasured memories for sure.

About the age of 10, I decided I wanted a bike and a local charity heard about this and donated a special bicycle that I could ride. OMG, I was over the moon – a bike that was mine.

Someone had the great idea of putting the brakes on the pedals, which meant that I could stop the bike by peddling backwards. The handlebars were padded and I rested my shoulders on them to steer. This gave me an amazing sense of freedom and for the first time I could ride my own bike to school. I loved giving my friends 'seaties' (where your friend sits on the back of the bike) home and sometimes I would be daring, sit up on my bike and announce, "Look, I'm riding with no hands!"

Around this time, I also started getting the feeling I was being looked over. I kept hearing a voice, which always said, "You're safe, we are here." I heard this if I felt scared, worried or troubled about things. I would never tell my mum or dad. In fact, I revealed this to no one. The voice was very loud in my head at times, and very, very powerful, too, but it always seemed to reassure me and it definitely made me feel safe. I often wondered where it came from and why I was the only one who seemed to hear the voice. I will tell you more about my spiritual experiences in my next book, as lots happened on my stay in Lourdes. I didn't know it at the time, but aged 14 I had a light-bulb moment upon visiting a grotto, but more about that later...

CHAPTER FOUR

School Time

I can remember the time when I started swimming lessons at school. I must admit I was scared. That's not because I didn't want to swim, but because I'd have to wear a swimming costume. I knew children from other schools would be at the pool and was worried about what they would say. I remember going in the changing room with all my female classmates. My good friend Shirley helped me to undress and put the costume on. I tried hiding my little stump, as I was starting to feel a bit self-conscious. At the same time, I knew I had to go swimming. I tried to hide behind my friends while the pupils from the other schools began to appear, but even so I did hear a few kids remarking that I had no arms and I saw them staring at me. But once they had gone, I was fine. The swimming teachers still wanted me to wear the armbands and came up with the idea of strapping about four of them around me with a bandage, which I must say I hated. My teacher, Mr Winston, said, "Let's try Mandy without the armbands as I think she will be OK and feel freer without them." OMG, I was so relieved! It wasn't long before I was swimming and receiving my blue stripe – a piece of blue ribbon that you could sew onto your swimming costume to show that you could swim a certain distance. I can remember feeling so proud to have it pinned to my red swimming costume, and I couldn't wait to tell Mum. I went on to receive my yellow and red stripes. Wow, I was so over the moon. But when it came to getting my white one I felt too unsafe when I got to the deep end and I lost my confidence every time.

I was delighted about receiving my stripes, but very disappointed about not getting the white one. I was so scared about not being able to feel my feet at the bottom of the pool. I used to worry about getting cramp, as I wouldn't be able to hold onto the sides. I would have loved to get all my stripes, but this time I was defeated and yep, I wasn't a happy bunny. I would have also loved to jump off the diving board, but OMG, no! I knew that was definitely not for me.

I also loved to join in when we had gym days at school. One of the exercises was to run up and down a bench while keeping our balance. Another involved wiggling plastic rings around our waist. The one thing I wanted to do but couldn't was to use the climbing frames and ropes on the walls. I had to watch my friends on them and that made me sad. I tried, but knew there was no way of being able to do these activities. I joined gymnastics and got my first gymnastics badge, which was another major achievement, but then I got bored and left.

I loved playtime and my friends and me would play a little game where we would dance around in a circle and sing, "I'm Shirley Temple, the girl with curly hair and two big dimples." I would get my little stump, lift up my skirt and say, "And I wear my skirts up there." OMG, we would show the boys our knickers and then run off. How funny was that!

My times at Woodside Infant and Junior schools were my best times in education. One thing I learnt to adapt to, which, thinking back, was strange, is not going to the toilet during the school day. I didn't want anyone to have to help me, so I must have psyched myself up to not want to go during that time – how odd. Also, before lunchtime each day, everyone had to go to the toilet and wash their hands. I can remember watching them do this, as I loved the smell of the little yellow bars of tar soap. I sometimes wished I had hands, so I could wash them, but I didn't let myself get sad about it, I just carried on with each day.

I also loved to join in with school games, such as rounders. I didn't need a bat to hit the ball with because I used the top of my foot. Boy, could I hit that ball hard – I loved it. Other favourites were long jump and running. I can remember trying hurdle jumping and I just couldn't get the courage to run and then jump the hurdle. Nope, I stopped every time – I just couldn't do it. Then there were our Christmas plays. The one that sticks in my mind was when I got the part as the main angel. Wow, my mum made me my outfit and I wore a white sheet with a tinsel silver belt and these big, beautiful angel wings. I also sported a silver tinsel halo around my head. I felt special, as I had to stand on the highest point on the stage and look down at Mary and Joseph. Ah, that is a special memory of mine. These were my best years at school, which ended when I went up to senior school. I was dreading it, as I knew there were going to be children there from other schools, which made me become very self-conscious about not having any arms. I even hid my little stump and wouldn't wear short sleeves anymore. I also said goodbye to my special fork and spoon, as I didn't want the kids I didn't know seeing me with them. I guess I started withdrawing, but I didn't tell my mum or dad. In fact, I told no one.

Another memory is of learning to deal with periods – yuk. I was at Roehampton when I was given these panty belts with what looked like a big hammock, i.e. sanitary towels, lol. These were thick pads with a loop at each end that you could hook onto the panty belt. OMG, what an uncomfortable thing to put between your legs and walk with. I hated it, and thank God pads with sticky tape were invented. Then I could stick the pad on my knickers and pull them up with the Wolfgang hook that had been specially made for me at Roehampton. May I say, what a brilliant idea it was to have one fitted to my toilet wall at home.

You may be wondering about the hook. Well, once again my dad came up with the genius idea of getting two coat hanger hooks and fitting them to a square piece of wood. One hook was left hanging so that I could use it to pull my knickers down. The other one was positioned the other way up so I could pull them up again. The hooks were screwed to the wall in our toilet and they amazingly meant I could take myself to the loo. One thing I really hated was having help in the little girl's room. I used to wear these thick, big blue knickers that you would wear for PE. I used my teeth to wiggle them up. To pull them down, I'd get my big toe in the knicker leg and yank them. Good job I was double jointed in both legs. But when I got to senior school, I didn't want to wear bloody big bloomers anymore, as I preferred smaller ones. This is where the Wolfgang toilet hook was used. It was fitted at the senior school just for me.

I will always remember starting my periods. I was only

11 and OMG, what a nightmare that was. On the morning I started them, I can remember running down stairs and saying to Mum, "I'm a woman now!" – lol. At the hospital in Roehampton they showed me the sanitary belt and told me to try it out. Well, blimey, it looked like a hammock with a massive thick sanitary towel in it. It was so uncomfortable and made my legs feel that they were wide apart, lol. Anyway, as time went on, thank God, sticky sanitary towels were invented. I just stuck them in my knickers and pulled them up with the help of the Wolfgang hook – yay.

I decided to try the arms again and asked my mum to get an appointment for me to get fitted with them. Another memory takes me back to when I was small and having to have body plaster casts made, which I hated. This man wrapped wet bandages soaked in plaster stuff around my top half. I then had to sit still until it became hard. Then he would come back and cut it all off.

They made me have these plaster casts for when I had new arms made. A jacket was made from the mould with arms on it. This was solid and was fitted over the top part of my body. It was awful and hard and in the summer, God did I feel uncomfortable. The sweat used to run from my head. I have to admit, I felt like a flipping robot.

At 11, my breasts had started to grow and I remember thinking, OMG, I can't have a strange man touching my boobs. At the same time, I knew I needed these arms because I wanted to be the same as all the other children. So I came up with a good idea. I said to my mum that when I went to have my plaster cast I would keep my bra on and the man could plaster over it. When we arrived at the fitting place for my artificial arms, the man came in and said I was to undress. Straightaway I told him that I was leaving my bra on. He didn't seem happy about it and said I could wear a body stocking, but I still said no. He explained to my mother that when cutting the plaster cast off he would have to cut through my bra at the back. I wasn't happy but it had to be done. I hated every wet bandage that was soaked in plaster of Paris and placed over my top half, especially as the man smoothed his hands all over it. Even worse was when he came to my breasts and I felt him touching them. I hated it so much, but I knew I needed to try the arms again.

Well, the day came for the fitting. My father had asked if the shoulder could be made more rounded, like how a dolly's arms were, as in the past I had looked more like a robot and had massive shoulders. So, they did this, and I must admit they looked much rounder, too. A gas cylinder was fitted in each arm, which made my hands open and close and the wrist spin. Whenever I pressed the tiny button fitted on one of my shoulders, I would hear a hissing noise. To be honest, I still felt like a robot, but I needed to give it another go. The day came when I wore them to school and my friends were excited to see what I looked like with arms. For the first few weeks, I liked them because I could write and sit like a normal person. Plus, I could wear skirts instead of trousers. Strangely, because I was left footed, I thought I would be left handed, too. So, the first time I put a pen in my hand, I put it in the left one. But this felt odd and so I tried the right hand. OMG, this felt so right – how strange. Anyway, after a few weeks I started feeling tired, as walking about from classroom to classroom with heavy arms on and two gas bottles was getting a bit much. Plus, some days

I just hated school. I know I shouldn't tell you this, but my friend and I would pretend that I needed the loo. We'd go in there and waste the gas out of my arms by opening and closing the hands. I would then go to the teacher and ask if we could pop home to get some more gas. We would go really slowly and by the time we got back, the lesson was over. Naughty, I know! Another strange thing is that throughout senior school I didn't do history, sing in assembly or do anything holy. How odd is that, especially considering what I now do for work?

I couldn't keep up at school. I was coming home very tired and I really wasn't happy. So, after two years, Mum found another school call Branwood, which was for children with different disabilities. I can remember going with my parents to look around the school. I really wasn't interested in any school, but I can remember seeing all sorts of children. Some were in wheelchairs, some had difficulty walking and, well, some looked normal. One girl was quite small with long blonde hair. She smiled at me when I went into the classroom that was going to be mine. Her name was Julie Archer and from that day on we were best friends. Julie had a hole in her heart and I will always remember how sometimes her lips would turn blue. However, I didn't know just how poorly Julie was or that her life was going to be cut short. My mum knew this, as Julie's mum Margaret used to speak to her about it. As well as a hole in the heart, she had blocked arteries. The doctors were shocked that Julie lived as long as she did, but she passed away in her mum's arms on 19th February, 1979. Bless her.

Now, as I settled in at Branwood and made more friends, this is the point I became a rebel…

CHAPTER FIVE

My Teenage Years

Where do I start? Well, I really didn't like school at all, but knew I had to go. I became very good friends with Julie and also Kay Newby. We were very close and into all sorts of things. I remember putting drawing pins on a certain boy's chair, and in Mr Lawson's class I would say to the girls, "Right, let's do nothing." And we did just that! It was funny at the time, but poor Mr Lawson thought we were a nightmare. I wanted to start a dance team and asked a few of the girls I liked if they wanted to be in my group. I wanted it to be a majorette group with twirling batons. We asked the head, Mr Harris, if we could do this and, in our breaks, we would make our hats and batons. He agreed and The Mandalettes were born. Oh, yes! We made tall, soldier-like hats with peaks and got sticks for batons, which we decorated with tassels at the end. The rest of the girls' uniforms were made up of white shirts and PE skirts. There were five girls – two of them my besties, Julie and Kay. I was the teacher and leader and boy did I make the girls march and twirl those batons.

Well, people got to hear about The Mandalettes and we were asked if we would perform our little show at a care home for the elderly called Bennett Lodge. By this time my group had gotten bigger, as some of my friends from my hometown had joined us. WOW, my dance group was big and every Saturday we would all meet up to practise our dance routines at a retirement home up the road from me called The Haven. I must say, my little sister Jane was a fantastic dancer and if I needed any new arm movements or a different style of baton twirling demonstrated, Jane was my girl. I did all the leg movements and dance routines myself – it was all teamwork. So, I said yes to showing off my dance team. Excited, or what? I will always remember the girls' first routine, which was to Neil Sedaker's *Calendar Girl*. I was so proud of them and we loved our first ever show. I knew I was a team leader and I was on a mission.

The strange thing is that when I look back at my schooling, I can clearly remember one particular assembly. We would all settle in the hall and Mr Harris's wife would play the piano. On this particular morning, I was giggling and being a bit naughty by refusing to sing the stupid hymns. Well, all of a sudden the piano stopped and Mrs Harris stared straight over to me and said out loud, "Mandy Hornsby, I've just about had enough of you. Every time we meet in assembly you distract the pupils and refuse to sing, so now get out!"

OMG, what an embarrassment. But I still gave off an attitude of *whatever*.

I now wonder what my problem was with holiness. I often speculate on why I wasn't into religious studies at school. Even when I went to Lourdes, I wouldn't pray or sing holy songs. Was I angry with God for allowing me to be born this way? Well,

I did question whether there was a heaven. Gosh, there must have been a reason. Considering what I do now for a living, it does baffle me. To this day, I do not know why I felt like that.

Anyway, by 14 years old, I had become a very grumpy girl with an attitude. What made matters worse was that Mr Lawson felt I was a ring leader with the girls in my class. On one particular morning, I was called to the head's office. *Oh no, what now?* I thought. Well, he told me to sit down and then said, "Mandy, you have been very hard work since starting this school and even my wife has tried with you. Now, Mr Lawson has asked for you to be removed from his class, as he feels you are stopping the other girls from working with your behaviour."

Oh my giddy God.

Then he said he had no choice but to put me in Mrs Larson's class. Now, I hated this lady in a very big way (sorry Mrs Larson) and I will always remember how she brought her snuffly little Pekingese dog to school with her nearly every day. She also had some snotty goody two-shoes girls in her class, whom I didn't like or even wanted to like. This is where I massively changed. I felt unhappy and really lost all interest in school. The only thing I really enjoyed was cooking lessons with Mrs Barnyard, whom we called 'Our Mrs B'. She was a lovely lady and taught me to cook. At Christmas, she helped me to make a beautiful cake that looked like a basket of fruit. I was so proud that I had made it – and all thanks to Mrs B. What peed me off, though, is that if ever Mr Harris had visitors to the school, it strangely seemed to be on my cooking days. He would come into the classroom and say, "Here's our Mandy. Now, Mandy, demonstrate how you crack eggs with your toes." This really peed me off big style and under my breath I'd say a few swear words, mostly beginning with f. At break times, I would meet with my trusted girls, Julie and Kay, along with two others I'd made friends with. They were called Susan Livermoor and Carina Green. We would go to the back of the field, which we called 'Our Corner' and bitch about everyone.

When it was home time, we would all have to get on a coach. Well, this was quite exciting and you are probably now wondering why. Well, the driver was a guy called Ray. Yes, he was an older man with a tash, but me, Julie and Kay loved him. We even got to sit at the front of the coach, just behind him. I had a thing about older men with a hint of grey. So, our morning and home time journeys were fun. One morning, we had a plan to get Julie to spray perfume over Ray as we got off the coach. We wanted his wife to smell it. I know that's not good, but back then we were just teenagers who wanted a laugh. When we got on the coach to go home, Ray wasn't his usual smiley self. Jean, his assistant, told us we'd been really naughty and that the perfume had gone into his eyes. He wasn't happy at all. Well, we were all made to sit at the back of the coach this time. On the journey, we all agreed to say sorry to Ray as we got off the bus at our respective stops. The next morning, we weren't sure about sitting at the front or if Ray would even smile at us again. I was nervous as I waited at the bus stop wondering where Kay, who go on first, would be sitting. When the bus pulled up, though, I could see her at the front behind Ray. Phew, everything was back to normal. Julie got on next and yay, we were back to having flirty fun again.

I can also remember hiding behind ponchos. When I was wearing one, I guess no one really knew I hadn't got any arms. Now, it seems really silly, but to walk down the street or in town with no one staring at me made me feel normal. Then some of my friends at school started wearing vest tops and I wanted to wear one, so Mum got one for me. But in no way would I wear it without a jacket. So, on one particular day, I wore my vest top with a black jacket. I remember thinking, *Oh, I have boobs, yes, boobs, and a nice cleavage too.* Lol. Then as we got into school, this boy came up to me and said, "Nice tits, Mand!" He then added, "I always wondered if you had tits and boy, they are nice." OMG, the ponchos were quickly made redundant!

Anyway, I got to hate school even more. One day, I went to the back of the field with my best buddies to have our daily meeting, and I said to them, "Girls, I'm not coming back to school – I'm just going to refuse." They seemed shocked and said, "It's not going to be the same without you here." I replied, "Don't worry, Kay will take over my place and if you need me, call me."

Every morning after that, I refused to go to school. I can remember my parents having a meeting with Mr Harris and asking if there was any way I could return to the class with my friends. They knew I had lost all interest since moving to Mrs Larson's. But the head said no. So, I said, "No, I'm never, ever going back." I stuck to that until the official leaving day, when I went back really just to wind a few peeps up, including Mrs Larson. It was sad though that Ray, our gawjuss coach driver, had by then left to work for another company. My school life had ended, thank God, but a deep depression was on its way.

CHAPTER SIX

My Darkest Time

Up until now, I had been a strong, happy-go-lucky kind of person and had managed to live a varied and normal life despite my disability. However, something shifted and BANG, the darkest cloud ever lingered over me. I was 14 and can't really remember much about it, as it's like a blank spot in my life. My mum said she started to notice I wasn't my usual happy-go-lucky self. Some days, I just sat in our garden on the swing doing nothing.

It was here that I think my seabed was beginning to overload and starting to unsettle, as I'd buried so many things. But I knew I couldn't allow my secret seabed to be disturbed, as I wasn't ready to deal with everything that I'd swallowed. I guess I managed to settle it once again, and this time I allowed a black cloud to float above my head. This made me want to be on my own and shut down my mind. It's a very blurry time. Even now, when I try to think back to that age, nothing comes up.

I think it was a time when my friends were getting boyfriends and talking boy talk. I guess at that age I thought no boy would ever fancy me, and I really hated my body then. My friends would ask me to go swimming with them and talk about wearing bikinis, and that made me feel sad inside. I also would have loved to wear my vest tops without a jacket, but I hated my very pointed shoulders and wanted to keep my stump hidden. Poor stumpy – lol. My friends wore rings and bracelets and painted their fingernails, which are things I would have also loved to join in with. So I guess I was creating this dark cloud over myself. My parents knew I loved horses and I'd been riding with the school a few times, so they decided to buy me my own little pony. Dad said they had found a little filly Welsh cob and that we could go and see her. WOW, excited or what! I remember going to this farm and a lady saying, "Come and meet Day Dream." Well, her full name was Dirkle Day Dream and there she was in this great big riding schoolroom. OMG, she was tiny and I loved her straightaway. Well, the time soon came for Day Dream to be delivered at Wilton Hall Farm, where my dad used to help out and do his shooting. From the age of 12, my dad had worked on farms and he loved shooting, which he still does now. The lovely owner, Tom Linsey, allowed me to keep my pony there. Also, my brother Robert worked on the farm and he lived there, too. Day Dream was waiting in her stable for me. I also went with Dad to buy her a leading rein, and guess what? It had to be red tartan as I was mad on the *Bay City Rollers*. So, Dad went into the stables, harnessed Day Dream up and brought her out to me. I remember Jane asking if she could ride her when she was older and I replied, "Maybe."

I think Mum and Dad thought getting the pony would help me come out of my depression. I never told them anything of what I was going through deep down, and one thing I would never, ever have done was to blame my mum or dad for being born the way I was. I just swallowed my sadness, like I did every time I felt hurt or sad about the way I was, and let it go into my seabed.

I dealt with it that way and now, as I'm writing my life story, it's like I've unsettled my seabed of deep, deep buried sadness. I've shed a few tears as I've typed and maybe it was time that my seabed was unsettled and cleared in order for my life to be fully complete, if that makes sense. I remember once having a chat with my mum and she said she used to have a recurring dream that she was chasing a pair of arms and trying to grab them for me – how awful. And she always worried that a day would come when I would turn round and blame her for being born with no arms. But I never did and to this day never would. I love my mum and dad so much and I'm proud of them both for making me strong.

I thought this dark cloud would go away and I could deal with it myself, but boy did I struggle to believe that at times. In the meantime, I couldn't wait until Day Dream was old enough to be broke in so I could ride her. Every day, I would go down to the farm and Dad would bring her out from her grazing field to meet me. She'd make a neighing noise and her ears would prick up and her nostrils would flare, so I knew she was pleased to see me, although she loved my dad and I guess she thought of him as her master. Well, the day came when Dad said it was time to sit on her and oh my giddy God, wow! I can remember asking Dad, "How do you know she won't buck me off?" He replied, "Trust me, she won't." Then he leant over her back and said, "Look, she's not moving, she's OK." My heart was racing and my legs were shaking. My dad picked me up and I slowly put my leg over her. She just turned her head round as if to say,

"What are you doing?" Then Dad said, "Come on, girls, let's walk." My heart was still beating fast as I wondered when she would buck, but nope, she just walked. I was shocked and loved it that I could now ride her every day. Wow, my own horse and she was all mine. It was now time to pick out a saddle, and I also wanted to get her shoed, but this is when tragedy struck. I remember this like yesterday. I was at home with my sister Sue. By this time her partner Fred had joined the farm and was working with my dad and Rob. I was in the living room when the phone rang. I heard my mum say, "Oh no, I don't know how to tell her." My sister Sue jumped up and asked in an upset voice, "It's not Fred, is it?" Mum came into the living room and said, "No, it's Day Dream." I'm crying as I type this, as my seabed has been unsettled once again. Mum added, "Day Dream is dead."

What? Oh no!

"I don't believe you," I said and started to cry. Mum called my dad and told him he better come home. I needed to know what had happened. Dad explained that there was a barn next door to Day Dream that was full of hay bales. She was being a bit greedy and put her head through the bars. As she pulled her head to get out, her back feet went and she strangled herself. My dad looked so upset, as he had grown to love her too. I said I wanted to go and see her but Dad said they had already buried her. I was so, so angry, but years later, Dad told me that the farm owner had her taken away. (I still don't know to this day where she went, but I'm assuming to a knacker's yard.)

I was absolutely devastated, because once I sat on her we had this connection. I was so excited to see her after school and the thought of being able to ride her made me really happy. Her death was really tragic and I suffered for a few months after. I felt I had lost a friend and also a hobby that had given me independence.

During the time I had Day Dream, I also developed a strange rash all over my body, which was very red and itchy. Mum took me to the doctors and he sent me to have some allergy tests to see if it was to do with my horse. I can remember receiving a row of pinpricks with different drops in them. One contained horsehair, another dust and then dog and cat hair. There were a few others, but they all came back negative. It was really odd having the tests done, as there were about 10 dots on my right leg and I had to wait to see if I had a reaction, but nope, not a thing. What on earth was this itchy rash? Boy, I remember getting a hairbrush and scratching myself till I bled.

Anyway, unbeknown to me, my mum got talking to a lady called Maureen Walsh, who was involved with a charity called Across. Mum told Maureen how worried she was about me, and how I had gone very deep, looked sad and still had this unidentified rash. Anyway, Maureen told my mum about the charity and how they took disabled people to Lourdes in France. She suggested to my mum that maybe it would do me the world of good and told her about the holy water, and many other things.

The next thing I knew, me and my little sister, Jane, who by then was about nine years old, were getting on this big, strange-looking coach. I'd been told I was going on a special break. Jane was quite excited but I was still as miserable as hell. I thought, *OMG, what has my mother done?* On the coach there were all sorts of people from young to old, as well as a nun. It was all so holy, holy, holy, and I wasn't a happy bunny at all. I noticed seats on one side of the coach and bunk beds with drawn curtains on the other. Jane couldn't wait to go to bed and she got on the top bunk, leaving me the bottom one. I still wasn't sure where we were going, though. Then we finally arrived at the Across chateau and me and Jane were told our accommodation was right at the top. It was a little attic room with two single beds and French doors that opened onto a small balcony.

Well, here goes my strange week. We visited different churches and oh my giddy God, why? Then we attended a service and Sister Ann, who was the nun helping us, said to Jane and me, "It's up to you if you want to join in." I replied. "What do you mean by that?" Well, straightaway, my very loud little sis said, "I will." Sister Ann explained that even though Jane and me were Church of England and not Catholic (and this was a Catholic service), we could still go ahead and have the bread and wine if we wanted. Jane said that she would, while I stormed out and sat outside in a wheelchair they'd got for me, as some of the churches we were visiting on our walking tours were up hills. The next thing I knew, people were walking by me and staring. They then started throwing me bloody money. *OMG*, I thought, *do I look like a Guy Fawkes dummy?* Lol. I was fuming, and the more I heard singing coming from the church, the angrier I became. I really wasn't happy with my mum at this time for making me go on this pathetic trip with holy and sick people. Anyway, the special day soon arrived. Again, I couldn't understand why everyone was so excited as they talked about Saint Bernadette and how the magic water happened and how holy it was. This was well boring to me at this stage in my life. So, I asked Sister Ann where we were going and she explained that they were taking me for a holy bath, where I would be dipped in holy water. She added that miracles can happen and told Jane and me a few stories of previous miracles that had happened for sick people. She added, "Maybe your rash will go, Mandy." Well, I thought in my head, *Yeah, whatever. Maybe a miracle will happen and I'll grow frigging arms, too!* I can remember being told off. They said, "You will love it, Mandy, now grow up." It was a bloody cheek telling me to grow up. I didn't even want to be there and I just couldn't get my head around why my mum thought this was going to be good for me. The only one enjoying the trip was Jane.

So, here we all were in this massive queue and there were very sick people in it, and even people who were dying. I felt sad and depressed as we waited for our turn. Then finally we were shown into this large room and oh my frigging God, there were loads of ladies in there, from young to old and from thin to fat. I hated it and even more so when we were told we were to take all our clothes off. Then, when it was our turn, we were to go into the next room where there were two nuns. They would help me into the holy bath and dunk me under. "Dunk me under what?" I asked Sister Ann and she explained that I would be submerged in the holy water. "It will feel cold at first, Mandy," she said. "So the nuns will wrap you in a sheet."

I was so angry and couldn't really understand all this crap, but I went along with it. I did, however, tell Sister Ann that I wasn't going to dunk my head under. So, off I went. I can remember stepping down the stone steps and into this water, which felt really strange. It was warm rather than cold and I was wrapped in this sheet and then told to get dressed without drying myself first. Jane, bless her, helped me to dress and the rest of the day was a blur.

The next morning, I got up early and snuck out. I found myself at the grotto. I was there by myself just standing and looking up at St Bernadette. I felt at peace, plus my rash had completely gone. Yep, gone. I was very shocked and I felt special, loved and calm, too. Then I went to look at this little stream nearby, and I know this is gonna sound crazy, guys, but as I looked at the water this big fish appeared and I felt I had a conversation with it. Yep, you may think I'm cuckoo now, but it was the most unbelievable feeling and very hard to take in. And that's not all. I then heard shouting. It was Jane and some others and they were cross with me. Jane told me I was in trouble and I replied, "Who cares?"

Anyway, that night, me and Jane went to bed and when she turned the light out, we could see the moonlight shining through the French doors. I couldn't sleep, as I just felt different inside and was still on a high from being at the grotto. Anyway, the next thing I knew – and again you're gonna think I'm crazy – the French doors swung open and OMG, my heart was thumping and I couldn't believe what was happening. A nun floated in through the doors. She had no face, hands or feet and I was scared and shouted, "Jane, put the light on, someone is in our room." She moaned at me, but got out of bed and put the light on. There was no one else there and the doors weren't even open. I was shocked and yes, Jane was not happy!

This is when I got my first intuition that I was connected spiritually. I kinda knew I was different, not because of having no arms, but because of these strange feelings, hearing voices and seeing things. I didn't want to tell anyone, not even my mum. I was worried in case they'd think I was going crazy. Every two years these voices kept coming back and wanting me to talk with them, but I shut my mind off. All I wanted was to be a normal Essex girl and get on with my life my way.

I didn't say anything the next morning and nor did Jane. I didn't really mix with the others and while Jane chatted with them, I wandered outside, where I heard someone whistling a tune. I went back in and saw this young guy painting the walls. He looked at me and smiled, so I smiled back. "Come in if you want, I'm Ben," he said. He said that he had noticed me a few days ago and asked my name. He then told me his father owned the place and that he was helping to paint the bedrooms. We started chatting and he asked how old I was. I must admit I lied – oops – and said I was 15. When I asked how old he was, he said he was 18. He invited me to have a look around the town with him that night and I said yes. OMG, I was so excited that he wanted to take me out. I can remember that we just walked around and chatted. He showed me all sorts of little places and we then sat down where people got together to sing holy songs while holding candles. I can remember hearing *Ave Maria* and thinking how beautiful it was. The next thing I knew, Ben put his arm around me and said, "You're very pretty." Then he kissed me. OMG, my very first kiss! I couldn't believe it. Then he said, "We better get back, as I said I wouldn't keep you out too late." When I returned, everyone was chatting in the living room. "Let's go to our room," I said to Jane, and I told her about my first kiss while we got ready for bed. That night I lay in bed thinking about Ben and that kiss. I couldn't wait to see him in the morning. Every day I would pop in and watch him paint and we would chat about loads of things. It was so sad when the time came to go home, but we promised to write to each other.

Back in England, I told my mum about Ben and how we were going to meet when he returned from France. Ben lived in Surrey, which wasn't far from Essex. I can remember writing to him and for a while I heard nothing. Then one day a letter arrived from him. I went upstairs with it under my chin, shutting my bedroom door and then opening the envelope with my toes. The letter was very long and in it he told me that although he thought I was a beautiful girl, he was too old for me and lived too far away. He didn't think anything could come of us meeting, as he had more work in France. My heart sank and I was very sad. I felt myself having to swallow my tears and sadness, letting them settle in my secret seabed once again. I couldn't wait for my mum to get my photos developed, as I had a few of me and Ben together, but when I did get them back the two pictures we'd had taken together were blurred. I was angry and sad, as when Ben and me were together we had chatted loads and I was in love with him. It was silly, but I guess this was my first love. I now know that Mum had been chatting with Maureen about Ben and me, and she'd said she was worried about me getting hurt. She also thought Ben was far too old for me. Mum only told me about this when I was 16, and we were having a long chat about my scary experiences with Spirit while I was in Lourdes. That's also when I told her that from the age of six, whenever I felt unsettled, I'd hear a voice say, "You're okay, you're safe."

I guess that when my mum told me about her concerns about my relationship, I felt her chat with Maureen had put an end to it, as nothing else happened. Maureen knew Ben and his father and I'm sure she relayed Mum's worries, which were to do with his age and also the fact that he was a Catholic and lived in both Surrey and France. I think Mum was just trying to protect me from someone older, so that I didn't get hurt.

I believe Ben came into my life for many reasons, particularly to prove to my 14-year-old self that I was pretty and that young men like Ben did find me attractive with no arms. I felt comfortable with him, and when he walked by my side and put his arm around me, it made me feel quite grown up. I can remember my heart beating excitedly and when he stopped and kissed me, well, erm, I just wasn't sure about having his tongue in my mouth – lol. I remember waking up the next day just wanting to see him and when I did my heart started racing excitedly again. And having a snog with no tongues was much better – lol.

After Lourdes, my mind changed and I became more confident because I knew I was pretty. It was time to see what was going to happen next. I loved wearing makeup and my hair had to be perfect. I came away from ponchos and started wearing vest tops with a jacket. As I've said before, I would never go out without a long-sleeved jacket. I guess I still hated my pointed shoulders. Oh, how I wished I had rounded ones with a bit of meat on them. But no, mine were like sharp pointed bones with no muscle or thick skin. And of course, I had no shoulder blades either. At least the vest tops showed I had boobs. I had a bloody good cleavage, even if I say so myself!

After I returned from Lourdes, the dark cloud seemed to lift and I went back to feeling positive again. I also felt that my secret seabed was at peace within me. I did feel different and I actually liked myself and wanted to dress up and feel attractive. Boy, did I change!

CHAPTER SEVEN

The Rebel

I began to feel pretty and started wearing make up and making sure my hair was always perfect. I couldn't wait to see my friends, Julie Archer and Kay Newby, and I also started up a friendship with a girl called Donna Netting, who lived just up the road from me. I can remember going to a few youth clubs but they weren't really my cup of tea. I was also friends with another girl called Tracey Tyson. I was now 16 and I received a letter from The Thalidomide Trust asking if I would like to go to London to be fitted up with an adapted car.

What? Wow!

I could hardly believe what I was reading and I couldn't wait to tell my friends. One evening, I was out with a mate when Dad called me to come in. He looked sad and then my mum said, "Sit down, we have just had the news that Julie has died." I replied that I didn't believe it and Mum said Julie's heart couldn't take it anymore. She told me that her mum, Margaret, had explained how Julie had blocked arteries as well as a hole in the heart. The doctors were surprised she had lived as long as she had. I knew she hadn't been well and Margaret had said that on the day she passed, on 19th February 1979, she had been getting very tired. I hadn't seen Julie since leaving Branwood. I went outside to my friends and cried as I told them the sad news. On the day of Julie's funeral, I remember seeing her sister Sandra, who hung around with us at the time. I remember going to Julie's home and her mum making us her gawjuss chips. We would sit in front of her fire to eat them. Julie loved a cup of tea with Digestive biscuits, which she called Favourites.

I remember another time in Julie's bedroom, which was filled with Donny Osmond posters and the colour purple, as Donny loved purple. We talked about growing up and what sort of boyfriends we would have. I couldn't believe that Julie had died. Her funeral was so sad and I held my head down all through the service and cried. I will never forget Julie Archer and I will love her forever.

My angel.

Well, the day of my appointment to go to London to be fitted with car adaptations and, of course, to pick a car, had come. So off I went with Mum and Dad to the capital. I was mega excited and still couldn't believe I was going to be able to drive. At the time, there were these little blue three-wheeler disabled cars on the road, but I'd always said I would never drive one of those ridiculous vehicles, as people would definitely know I was disabled. I was lucky because I was never offered one of these. Anyway, I got called into this room where there was a half built car. I was then told to sit in it. I thought, *OMG this is stupid*. I asked the guy why I needed to do this and he said they had to test my reflexes. They told me that on their instruction, I needed to brake as quickly and as hard as I could.

Then they showed me the foot steering that would move the steering wheel. They asked me to put my left foot in this stirrup and turn the footplate. To my amazement, the steering wheel turned on its own. Wow and even more wows!

I couldn't believe that I was going to learn to drive. I had a choice of two vehicles – a MINI or a MINI Clubman Estate. I went for the Clubman, as it was bright red. Anyway, I had to wait months before the car was adapted and I just wanted it to hurry up.

Meanwhile, my dad came home from work one afternoon and said he had asked his boss, John Spurge, if he would give me a job in the office at Bisons. This wouldn't be my first job, as for a short time while at school there was a work experience programme. I applied to do mine at a florist in my local town. But when they found out about my disability, they said there was really nothing they could offer. Another time, I got friendly with a girl across from where I lived called Lyn Lee. She worked in her dad's pet shop and poodle parlour. I started talking to her every day and she asked me if I fancied having a go at serving in the shop. She said she was sure I could do it, and bloody hell I felt excited. When someone came in and wanted some birdseed weighed up, I'd put a brown paper bag on the scales and use my feet to scoop the seed into the bag. I'd use my feet again to get the bag onto the counter and I'd take the money with my toes. Well, I actually found I enjoyed doing this and Lyn said I could help her every day if I wanted. OMG, I felt that someone could finally see past my disability. One morning, Lyn's dad popped into his shop and watched me work. He was called John Lee and he knew both my parents. He just let me carry on and he also asked if I was enjoying myself. I replied, "Oh, yes, I can't believe you're allowing me to help out." He said that all that mattered was that I was enjoying myself. I even swept up, too, by putting the broom handle under my chin. It was easy-peasy, lol.

Now, my parents got talking to Lyn's dad and he said he was selling up. My parents knew I enjoyed working in his shop so my mum thought that if they took the shop on it would be a job for me. So, my parents became the owners of Thurrock Poodle Parlour. Mum trained herself up by watching the dog clipper at work. Boy, was she a quick learner. I couldn't believe how good she became. Meanwhile, my dad worked in the pet shop. The sad thing is, though, that as soon as my parents took over the shop I totally lost interest in it and didn't want to work there.

So, that's when my dad decided to ask his boss about giving me a job, which he did. I can remember my first day in the office. God, I was nervous. Dad took me in to meet his boss, John, who was so lovely. He said that Margaret, who worked next door, would show me what to do. "Just let me know if there's anything you need," he added. Meanwhile, my dad took my Wolfgang toilet hook in and had it fitted in the ladies' toilet.

Anyway, the day finally came and I got the letter saying my car was ready to pick up – whooohooo! So, the British School of Motoring took me to collect my car and I took Julie Archer's sister Sandra with me. If Julie were alive, I would have taken her.

We were picked up by a guy called Gary. He was going to be my driving instructor. I was so excited and just couldn't wait to pick up my very own car. Gary said to me on the journey that he had never taught anyone without arms before. "To be honest, I'm a little nervous," he confessed.

Oh, thanks, Gary, great start! I thought, lol.

Sandra thought he was quite nice looking. Anyway, there it was – a very bright red MINI Clubman Estate. It was mine – oh, yes – all mine. All I kept thinking about was the freedom and independence. Soon I would be able to go out on my own. I must admit, I did ask for dark windows, as I didn't want anyone to see me driving, but the company said no. Anyway, the day came for my very first driving lesson. Gary turned up, got out this stupid big cone, with BSM written on it, and placed it on top on my car. "OMG, do I have to have that on my car?" I asked. "'Fraid so, Mandy," Gary replied.

Sandra was allowed to come with me once again, and she excitedly got into the back. We all got comfortable and Gary explained that he had a brake set up in the passenger side. Well, I started my car with the key that was fitted to a box on the floor at my right side. The box also contained light and window switches. My indicator switch was fitted on my accelerator. All the adaptations were cool and they amazed me. My heart was racing as I placed my left foot in a stirrup that was fitted to a flat plate, which moved the steering wheel. Amazing. Well, we were off. Oh my giddy God, I was driving. I really felt that Gary was a bit scared, like me. Anyway, he was only my driving instructor for a few times and then I was introduced to another guy called Steve. Wow, I must say what a good-looking man he was. Anyway, he was very excited and confident too. As time went on, I got very good at driving and I'd also started to fancy Steve. Well, on one particular day we went for a night lesson and afterwards pulled up at a pub. "Shall we have a drink?" Steve asked. My heart was beating excitably as Steve went into the pub to get the drinks while I waited in the car. We sat chatting about things and he stroked my long hair and said I was very pretty. Then, whooohooo, we were kissing. I couldn't believe I was actually having a bloody good snog with my driving instructor. I couldn't wait to call my friends the next day. I phoned my best friend Donna Netting and told her all about my kisses with Steve. I was so excited inside but didn't say anything to my mum and dad. OMG, I just couldn't believe how attractive and normal I felt, if that makes sense. Donna was younger than me and still at school. We used to chat about losing our virginity and how scared we were. Donna was at an all-girls convent school. I couldn't wait to pass my driving test, as me and my friends had plans to go all over the place.

Above: Me and my mum - The Sunday Times came to do a story on me.

Below: Me showing off! Choccy biccie anyone? Lol.

Above: Photos of me taken by The Sunday Times.

Below: The doctors said I would never stand, let alone write and play like any other child.

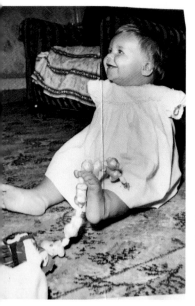

Above: Me and my mum at my 2nd birthday. I was determined to cut the cake!

Below: The dreaded robot arms!

Above: The editor of the Thurrock Gazette, presenting me with a bicycle.

Below: Me with my niece (with my arms on!) and me brushing my hair.

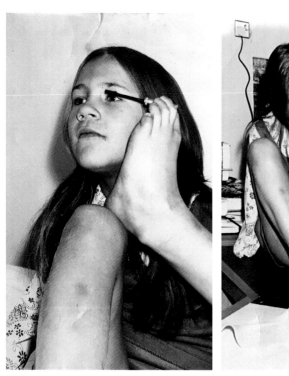
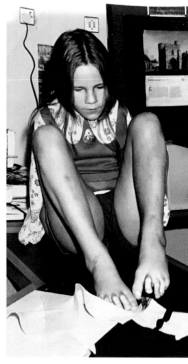

Above: Putting on makeup and cutting material with some electric scissors.

Below: Me and my sister Jane's school photo.

Above and Below: Me and Day Dream, such a lovely and gentle pony.

Above: Me and my sister Jane at Southend Airport flying to Jersey.

Below: Waiting to get onto the Across Jumbulance coach, off to Lourdes.

Above and Below: The Chadwell Mandalettes - I was part of the troop when I was 13.

Above: Members of the The Mandalettes in our uniform.

Below: Me twirling my batons and featuring in the Thurrock Gazette.

MANDY at 16, twirling her majorette batons.

Above: Me and Manfred in Switzerland, and me rollerskating!
Below: Me and my friend Donna - out and about!

Above: Me and my sister Jane (and Sandra and Tina) with my Mini.

Below: Me and Mandy at the Black and White Nightclub in Switzerland with DJ Chris. Me with Willy Critchlow and Mark Bond

Above: Me, my sister Sue, my sister-in-law Sue, and Donna.

Below: Me with gawjuss Wayne at a beer festival.

Above: My magical wedding day!

Below: The vicar couldn't believe I could sign the register! Me deep in thought before I said "I do!" lol.

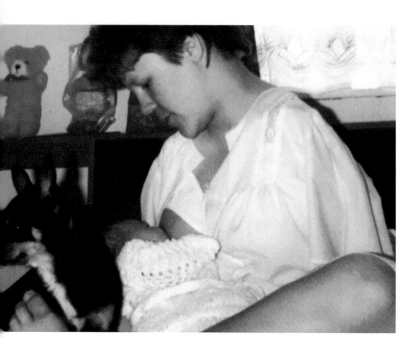

Above: Me feeding Nicola - easy as!

Below: Cradling Marie with my legs.

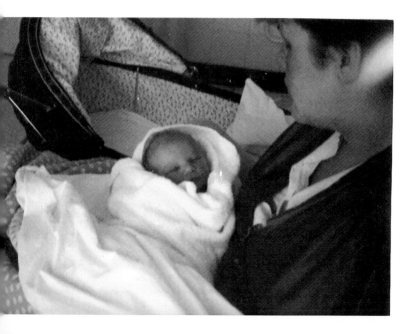

Above: Both of my girls, Nicola and Marie.

Below: Me and Nicola with my 'just for show' arms. I hardly wore them, but it was so sweet that Nicola wanted to hold my 'hand'.

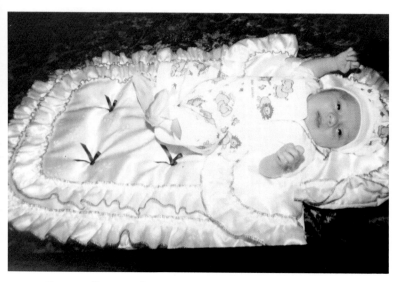

Above: Callum, my first grandchild. I was the first thalidomide grandmother.

Below: Me and Mumsie xxx

CHAPTER EIGHT

Meeting Other Thalidomides

I remember this particular day quite well. My mum had mentioned that the Thalidomide Trust had arranged a holiday to Switzerland for thalidomide people. Mum asked if I wanted to go. I must admit, I had never really wanted to meet other thalidomides and there had been many holidays I could have gone on that I turned down. Anyway, I thought, *Yep, I'm gonna give this a go*. So, the day arrived and I was all packed. Me, my mum and dad and my sister Jane went up to Heathrow Airport. My fantastic dad had made me another device to help me pull my jeans and knickers up, as I wanted to be able to fully dress myself. He put a coat hanger hook on the end of a long wooden stick and then put black tape around the top, which I put in my mouth. I'd then use the hook to pull either my knickers or my jeans up. I also had a small hook on a stick that I'd use to pull my zips up and down too, and a button hook from the hospital in Roehampton. So I was all equipped for being independent. My mum said, "Don't worry if you can't do everything, as there will be helpers going on the holiday to assist you if you need it." Anyway, we arrived at a Heathrow hotel and OMG, as we were shown to the bar where all the other thalidomide people were, I was shocked, and I mean shocked. I had never seen anyone like me before, and to see some folk with no arms or legs made me very sad. "I've changed my mind," I said to Mum. "I want to go home." Mum replied, "Stop being stupid, Mandy, you'll be OK when you start talking to them." Mum must have had a word with one of the helpers, as this woman came over – I can't remember her name, just that she had red hair – and invited me to come and meet the others. I reluctantly went with her and sat down. I just couldn't believe what I was seeing. Some people had little hands at the end of their shoulders and some had no arms or legs at all. A few were smoking and swearing. I must have looked so stuck up in comparison. Then I was introduced to another girl, who was also called Mandy. She was deaf and although she had arms, her hands were deformed. In my head, I thought, *Frigging hell, how can I communicate with someone who is deaf?* Then the helper women said, "You two are sharing a room." Oh, great. I went over to my mum and said, "I ain't stopping here. I don't have anything in common with these guys – not a thing." I was fuming. My mum and dad said, "Stop behaving like a child. You're 16 and acting like a five year old." And then my cheeky sister, who was now 12, said, "I'll go." Anyway, my mum and dad told me they were going. OMG, my heart sank, just like it had when I went to Lourdes. Anyway, Mum said to me after that it was so hard making the decision to walk out of the hotel. Meanwhile, I just sat there not talking to anyone. "She'll be OK," my dad said, and they left. Well, as I sat in the bar with all these very odd people, a young guy came up to me and said, "Ya alright then?" He asked my name and said he was called Willy and that he was from Newcastle. I found it hard to understand him at first, but I must admit I thought he was quite good looking. Willy was also thalidomide, but he just had deformed hands. He dressed quite cool, too, in all jean gear, and he had quite long hair. Anyway, the helper woman came over and introduced me to another girl – yet another Mandy. She had the same deformities as Willy and was from Birkenhead in Liverpool. She also had a strong, strange accent, lol. I had only ever really heard Essex people, as I hadn't mixed much with people from other parts of the country. Anyway, Mandy and me clicked straight away and asked if we could share a room. The organiser said not at the hotel, but we could when we got to Switzerland. I then thought, *Thank God, as in no way can I communicate with someone who is deaf.* Although the other Mandy was really nice, we just didn't gel. Well, as I lay in my bed at the hotel, I just kept thinking about how different I was to the others and how in some ways I was so lucky just to have been born with no arms. I started to feel really upset about the others and must have cried myself to sleep that night.

CHAPTER NINE

Switzerland Changed My Life

Well, we all arrived at The Hotel Goldie in Interlaken, central Switzerland, and me and Mandy couldn't wait to get our room. It was snowing and after a few days we decided to sneak out one morning and spend the day together. It was naughty, but we wanted a bit of fun. We went to a restaurant and ordered a curry, which was lush. We also had a few drinks. I had never really tried alcohol before and went for a Pernod with black current. OMG, it was strong, but also lovely. Well, we had an amazing afternoon and dreaded going back to the group, coz we knew we were going to get a telling off. Anyway, every night we all went to this nightclub and danced the night away. It was amazing and yep, I was getting drunk on the Pernod. I was also becoming good friends with Willy. It was nice getting dressed up every night and going to the nightclub. I was enjoying just being myself. I also started swearing, which I had never really done at home. I can remember one night being really, really drunk and feeling sick. I was hanging my head over the loo waiting to throw up when Mandy asked if I wanted her to put her fingers down my throat to help things along. I had to laugh and said, "No, but thank you." I became more confident on the holiday and I didn't even mind eating out. I had never been to a restaurant before so I was dreading going to one, as I was worried about the tables being too high for me to get my left foot up onto. Plus, I thought people might stare when I started to use my feet. But when Mandy and me first went out and had that curry, I really didn't care – I just felt good. In the daytime, we would visit different places and even went on a ski lift that went up very, very high into the snowy mountains. There was also a revolving restaurant that was once was used in a James Bond film, and we had a wonderful meal there, too. It was nice talking with other thalidomides and hearing their life stories. I'd always thought I was the only one, lol.

We then all decided to try ice skating. OMG, how funny was this? I was only on the rink for a little while and bang, I fell and landed right on my bum. I started to cry and was in extreme pain. The next thing I knew, I was in an ambulance going to hospital.

Months back, I had fallen down the stairs at home, as I rushed to get ready for work. I had gotten up late and I fell, or should I say bounced, down every step, from top to bottom. As a result, I fractured my coccyx bone at the bottom of my spine. Boy, was that a painful thing to fracture. While skating, I had fallen on my bum again and fractured it. God, it was so painful. I had to rest back at the hotel for about four days. I lay in bed while everyone else went to the nightclub. Willy stayed to keep me company and we became girlfriend and boyfriend. I really didn't want to go home. Mandy said we would go to Switzerland again, but this time it would just be me and her. When we landed at Heathrow, my parents were waiting for me. Mum said she could hear my voice before she could see me. She was shocked that I was swearing very loudly and she noticed that I had changed a little. Considering I hadn't wanted to go on the holiday, I now didn't want it to end. I felt ready to party and wanted to have fun.

As I got older, my seabed wasn't too bad. I started to accept myself and I voiced my opinions quite strongly…if I wanted to be gobby, I was. I still had the seabed, but I knew that all that crap from when I was younger had settled deep inside me.

Mandy and I started talking on the phone and decided we wanted to go back to Hotel Goldie, just me and her this time. So, about two months later we did just that. Our parents couldn't believe that we were ready to travel together on our own, but I needed to prove I could do things independently. Well, we were dropped off at the airport and we were off – how exciting. The only fear I had to overcome was bloody escalators. I was fine going up but had a big problem coming down. God, it took me ages to get on the first one and there were a few we had to go on at the airport in Switzerland. Anyway, we got to the hotel and the staff there remembered us from before and treated us well. Mandy and I couldn't wait to go out, so we got dressed up and went to have fun. Before going to the nightclub, we'd go to a little café for a pre-clubbing drinky poo. It wasn't just a café – it had a bar too. Anyway, I always had a Pernod and black and Mandy loved her beer. That night, as we were chatting, I noticed this gorgeous guy across from us. He had the most perfect hair and a little tash too. He wore a leather bomber jacket and very tight jeans. OMG, he had such gorgeous brown eyes. Well, every night he would be sitting in the corner, same time and same place. One evening he smiled at me, so I smiled back.

Then, as me and Mandy were leaving to go to our usual club, we noticed him leaving at the same time. And guess what? He was going in our direction. He then came into the nightclub, got a drink and – whoohooo – sat at our table. The sad thing was, he didn't speak a lot of English. Anyway, I asked his name and he said Manfred. OMG, what a name. Anyway, Mandy and me explained that we both shared the same name. I'm not sure he really understood, lol. But the one thing that was clear was that he was drop dead gawjuss. Anyway, every night Mandy and me followed the same routine. We got dressed up, stopped at the little café and then danced the night away at the Black and White Nightclub. And yes, Manfred started coming with us, too. Boy, could he kiss. I managed to understand that he was a hairdresser in his father's salon. It was really sad when it was time to go home. I can remember Manfred walking us back to our hotel. I sat outside with him. There wasn't a lot of talking going on, just lots of kissing. He had such beautiful eyes and the next thing I knew he was crying. "What's wrong?" I asked. He said that he was sad I was going home. Ah, bless, but I had to go. I tried telling him that as soon as we got home, Mandy and me were going to book to come back, and I hoped he understood. Well, as soon as we arrived back in the UK, Mand was booking the next trip to Switzerland. We couldn't get into the Goldie, but we had made a friend there called Doris, who was very pretty, worked in reception and spoke very good English. I called her and asked if she knew of another hotel nearby. She found us one that was actually closer to the lovely little café where I'd met Manfred. Anyway, as soon as our cases were emptied, they were being packed again. I don't think my parents could believe I was doing this on my own and feeling on top of the world.

Here we were back in very, very snowy and cold Switzerland, but we loved it. I couldn't believe how thick and heavy the snow was this time. The hotel that Doris had found us was perfect and as soon as we settled in, we got dressed up to go out. I was so excited and couldn't wait to see if Manfred was going to be in the same corner of the café, and at the same table. Well, there we were drinking our usual round of Pernod and black for me and a beer for Mand. Time was getting on and sadly there was no Manfred. I felt a bit sad really, but Mandy said, "Come on, let's party." So off we went. At the nightclub there was a group of guys who were all absolutely gorgeous. We got talking to them and they told us they were in the army. They were a great bunch and they did ask Mandy and me to go back to their hotel and party, but we said no. We didn't really know them and you never know what could have happened. Mandy got talking to this guy called Daniel. He had blonde hair and a tash and was quite a strapping lad. He also spoke better English than Manfred. Anyway, on the second night, we went to the café and who should walk in? Manfred! OMG, he looked so shocked to see us sitting there. Anyway, to cut a long story short, we all ended up going to the club, where we met Daniel and became a foursome. Daniel helped me communicate with Manfred. I discovered that he had a girlfriend and that his father wanted them to marry, but Manfred said he wasn't ready to tie the knot. He had known this girl from a young age and he didn't want to disappoint his father. At the time, I really didn't care. I was out for fun and excitement and Manfred was such a good kisser. I must admit, I didn't want to be a virgin, but oh my giddy God, I was a bloody scaredy-cat, lol. I was just too scared to go further, as I was only 16 and Manfred was in his twenties.

He must have wondered why I wouldn't go further, especially as I had also told him that I was 18. Just a little white lie – oops.

One morning, Mandy and I went for a horse sleigh ride. It was lovely. When we got into the sleigh we were covered in a warm blanket and were given a tour of the snowy town. As the horse trotted, the bells on his reins tinkled. It was just wonderful and it reminded me of Christmas. Then we had a nice meal and yep, we went out on the town once again. One afternoon we were a little fed up so I dared Mandy to dress up in her fishnet tights, high-legged stiletto boots and mini skirt. Mandy had this leather jacket with tassels under the arms. It reminded me of a rocker's jacket, so I dared her to go out dressed in the entire outfit and OMG, she did! The snow was falling mega hard as we walked to the little café. How Mandy could walk in them high boots I'll never know. Anyway, on the way back to our hotel it was getting dark and we noticed that a very strange little man was following us. "We better hurry up and get back," I said to Mandy. "He looks like a dirty old man." Well, we started walking faster, but the snow was falling even heavier now. Mandy slipped and slid all over the place. Although we were a bit scared we also pissed ourselves. Phew, we finally got back to the hotel. As we reached the safety of its doors, we realised the dirty old man had disappeared. We couldn't get into our room quick enough. What an experience, but fun too.

Once again, our time in Switzerland had come to an end. Mandy had to say goodbye to Daniel and I bid Manfred a tearful farewell. I guessed that it was the last time we'd ever see them, and Switzerland.

CHAPTER TEN

A Bleak Blip

Now that I had started living life and had come to the realisation that I could attract guys, I wanted more fun. Donna became my bestie and I confided in her about everything. We got together whenever I arrived home from my exciting holidays, and the first thing I'd say was, "I'm still a virgin!" Lol. Anyway, Donna and me got friendly with two brothers called Georgie and Stuart, who had just moved onto our street. But then a rumour went round that the family wasn't good and we were told by both sets of parents not to go to their house. Well, when you get told don't you do. Well, I did anyway – and Donna, too. I had a thing with Georgie and Donna got with Stuart.

The darkest moment in my life, apart from when I was 14, occurred around this time. I was starting to rebel against my parents and was hanging around with people they didn't want me to see. When I got told, "You're not going out," or "You're not to hang around with them," well, it got my back up and I thought, *Um, whatever, I'll do what I want.* There were a few other personal family things going on, which I won't go into here. But it was as if my mind overloaded and bang, I didn't want to be on this earth anymore. I'd had enough.

I can remember having so many arguments with my parents. My dad was so angry when he found out I was over at the boys' house, but by this time I had a very big attitude and my mouth was a bit foul, too. I can remember telling my mum and dad to f-off and saying, "I'll do what I want." Well, on this particular day, I was grounded because the night before I hadn't come in by a certain time so my dad had come looking for me. Yep, he found me at that house. He was fuming. Donna got into big trouble, too. On this particular Saturday morning, I was very moody and had a big row with my little sister Jane, who had been trying to wind me up. My eldest sister Sue was downstairs with her hubby Fred, talking to my mum and dad. God, I was in such a mood and was arguing with everyone. To this day, I still don't remember taking the tablets. Yes, tablets. I must have got into such a rage! I can remember shouting at my mum and dad and saying I hated everyone and wanted to leave home. I can recall being upstairs and me and Jane proper arguing. We had a little fight too, as my legs could give a mean old kick when they wanted to, and I always used to kick Jane right up the arse, lol. Anyway, as I came downstairs, she threw one of those square double plugs at me, which hit my foot. I just felt that no one was listening to me. All I remember is standing on a stool in the kitchen and reaching the top cupboard with my left foot. I had to balance on my right leg to do this. It's hard to imagine, but believe me – I had very good balance. The next thing I remember is going into the living room, where my mum and dad were still talking to Sue and Fred. I was clutching an empty bottle of pills in my left foot. I can't remember undoing the bottle or even putting any tablets in my mouth, but I do remember saying to my mum, "See, I've done it!" And I held the bottle up and chucked it on floor. Then I went upstairs and got into bed. My mum and dad came rushing upstairs and Dad said, "Have you taken them?" I just said, "Go away and let me sleep." My dad asked my mum how many tablets were in the bottle, but she couldn't remember. They kept shouting at me, "How many have you taken, Mandy?" But all I wanted to do was sleep. The next thing I remember is seeing my brother Rob at the end of my bed. He too kept asking how many tablets I'd taken. Then my mum phoned Donna and got her to come round. And, of course, an ambulance was on its way. As I started to drift off to sleep, I realised Donna was sitting on my bed crying. "Mand, Mand, how many did you take?" she asked. I told everyone to go away. In fact, I actually ordered them to f-off. All I wanted was to die and for them to let me sleep. Then I heard two ambulance men come into the room. They weren't sure how to pick me up. By this time, I was agitated and I was telling them to leave me alone and using the f-word over and over. Poor Donna was sobbing and saying, "Don't die, Mandy." When I think back it makes me feel really sad. I wonder why I did it and why I don't remember actually putting the pills in my mouth.

I also wonder why I would want to die, as I was just discovering myself, having fun and getting to like who I was. So why did I do something so stupid? Anyway, there I was in a hospital room. They put a tube down my throat and flushed my stomach out. It was the most awful thing I'd experienced in my life. OMG, just awful. I was crying, gagging and moaning. Well, that night I was monitored throughout. A nurse kept checking my pupils. In the morning, I was so grumpy that I didn't want to talk. I didn't even want any breakfast. All I wanted was to go home. Then a doctor visited and asked why I'd taken the pills. "I didn't take any pills," I replied. "Yes, Mandy, you did. We found them in your bloodstream. That's why we pumped your stomach last night." I simply refused to talk to him anymore. I also didn't want to see my mum or dad. I wanted no one and felt very down and angry. But my parents were coming anyway, and as I waited for them the nurses sat me in a wheelchair in the TV room. I remember looking out the window and thinking about nothing at all. Then this lady came in and said she was here to help me, and if I wanted to talk about things she was like a counsellor. I just stared at her. She kept asking if I was having problems at home and I just looked at her and told her to f-off. God, I wasn't a nice person and I just wanted to be left alone. Finally, my mum and dad walked in. I didn't say anything, but I noticed that they both seemed sad. "Are you ready to come home?" Dad asked.

It took a few days before I really said anything and no one questioned me or even asked me why I'd taken this vow of silence. Donna came to visit and we went into my bedroom. "Oh, Mand," she said. "I thought you were gonna die." I just laughed and said, "It's over now, Don, so where are we going tonight?"

Getting over what I had done took me about two weeks. My seabed was still lingering so I swallowed the situation and it was gone, thank God. Life went on as usual and only certain peeps knew I had tried to end my life. My dear Donna never asked me why, she was just so relieved I was alive. Even to this day, I still can't remember swallowing a full bottle of capsules.

I can remember carrying the empty bottle in my left foot, throwing it in the living room and even saying, "There, I've done it!" I can also recall getting into my bed and just wanting to sleep. Gosh, how sad is that? And how weak-minded of me.

CHAPTER ELEVEN

My Freedom

Anyway, my driving test was here and I was so excited. Thinking back now, I was a bit too sure of myself, and yep, I failed. OMG, sad or what!? But on the plus side, that meant I had a few more lessons with Steve and then I took my second test, which I did pass. Yaaaay. The first place I drove to was my sister Sue's. The feeling of getting in my car on my own and driving was one of complete freedom. Then I decided to pick Donna up from her convent school. I remember parking right outside, with music blaring. When I saw Donna walking out, I bibbed my horn and she came running over. Her first words were, "Have you passed, then?" Lol. I replied, "Of course, Don, otherwise I wouldn't be sitting here, duh." Anyway, that night Donna and I went cruising around, and it was brilliant.

Meanwhile, Mum heard about another holiday set up by the Thalidomide Trust. They now had a place on Jersey, in the Channel Islands, where all the thalidomide people could go if they wanted a break. Well, I decided to go and take my younger sister Jane with me. What an experience. I met up with Willy, whom I had been seeing in Switzerland, as well as lots of other thalidomide people. The place was called Haigmoor and it was so cool. There were loads of rooms downstairs and two rooms that you could either watch TV in or play pool. One of the smaller rooms had been turned into a bar and there was a lift to more rooms upstairs. There was also a swimming pool, and at the bottom of the garden was the beach. So, yep, it was a cool place full of teenagers drinking and smoking. They were all thalidomide people and everyone had either a family member or a helper with them.

Anyway, me and my sis were introduced to the managers, John and Jean Bennett. At first we thought they were really nice, but as we settled in and made friends, we all got a bit too rowdy. On this particular day, everyone was playing around the pool and the boys kept chucking us into the water with our clothes on. Well, me and Jane just used to throw our wet clothes on our bedroom floor. The cleaner complained to the manager. Anyway, he called me and Jane to the office, which was more like the naughty room, and started having a moan. Jane was quite a cheeky girl and started having a moan back. So did I. It was quite funny really, coz John Bennett – JB – turned round to both of us and said, "Any more cheek and both of you will be sent home." You had to laugh, really, as when we'd had a few too many drinkies, we all became cheeky and naughty and very wild. Some nights you could hear the doors shutting as people went to each other's rooms for you know what, lol. This holiday place was all about sun, sea and sex. Fun, fun, fun, but I have to say that yep, I was still a bloody virgin.

When I got back from this crazy, wild and fun holiday, I had to laugh coz Donna asked, as usual, "Well, are you?" I laughed and replied, "I still didn't have the guts." We often talked about losing our virginity, but I just couldn't imagine doing it with anyone. Well, I had made some friends in Jersey who hailed from Brighton. They were called Steve, Stuart and Frankie. They asked if me and a few of my mates wanted to go to Brighton for a party. Oh yesssss, a party. So I asked my friends Sue Livermoor and Tracey Tyson, as well as my bestie, of course, Donna. But because Donna was the baby in the group (only 16), I had to go round to her house and ask her dad if she could come with us. He said she could go, but she wasn't allowed to stay out all night and was to be indoors by 1am at the latest.

Well, how excited were we? Oh yes, Brighton here we come. I loved dressing up and every Saturday, Donna and me would get on a bus to Romford and I would shop, shop, shop. Poor Donna carried all my bags, bless her.

Anyway, I picked all my mates up and off we went with the music blaring. We were so bloody excited. Well, we arrived and met the lads. It was only a small party, and Sue had a little thing going on with my friend Stuart. We were sitting in my car, with Sue and Stu having a little snog, and all of us having a good laugh with the lads, when I noticed the time. It was 12.30am. OMG, I'd forgotten that Donna had to be back by 1am. I will never forget the journey home. The girls had all had a little drinky and I'm not sure how seriously they took it when I said to them, "My petrol is very low and if we don't find a petrol station we are gonna be stranded." Finally, I found one, but bloody hell it only took pound notes, as the actual garage was closed. Every time Donna put one in, the machine spat it out, as the notes were too screwed up. OMG, the time was now 1.30am. Donna was panicking and finally, after the long drive home, we got her back about 2ish. Boy, her dad wasn't happy with me.

Let the fun life begin. Now, one thing I'm not proud of is that I started to drink and drive. Looking back now, I realise what a stupid girl I was. But it was my first time feeling really free and I loved my car. But if my girls…if my girls had done this, I would have gone mental. To think my parents couldn't stop me, as I was in and out. My God, the worry they must have felt. Why did I want to rebel? What was the purpose? I am thinking as I type and contemplating how many lives I could have put at risk. I do feel ashamed to tell you this and even typing it now, I feel very sad about what I put my dear parents through.

I used to get ready and be out the door by 7pm to pick up all my mates. We crammed even more into my tiny estate and off we'd go for fun and adventure.

My friend Tracey knew of this gay pub in East Ham and we were told that on a Saturday night this old man in his sixties performed a striptease. OMG, well, you know, lol! "Lets go and find this pub," I said to my mates. I had never seen a gay person before. So off we went. I can remember saying to Donna, Tracey and Sue, "I hope they don't think we are lezzas, guys." Anyway, we found the pub and went in. Well, I just couldn't believe it. There were girls snogging girls and wow, some bloody good-looking guys snogging guys. When we were up at the bar, we made it quite clear that we were straight, but you know what, all the peeps were so friendly and lovely. Anyway, the stripper came on stage. Well, OMG, he was old – yuk. And when he lit some little fire sticks, he managed to set his pubic hair alight. Oh, bless his little cotton socks. We started going up there every Saturday night, but I daren't tell my parents. One evening, I got talking to this guy called John. He asked to take me out, but, um, the only thing was that I was 17 and he was 32. I must admit, though, I did have an attraction for older guys. "Yeah, why not," I told him. But first I asked him if he was gay. He said no, lol. Well, we started seeing each other. I knew no one in my family would approve of this relationship, as John was much older. I think that once again I was doing what I did best, and that was to rebel and wind my parents up. I thought I knew best and being with a much older man with a car was brilliant. I got John to pick me up one night outside my house. Wrong! Yep, my little sis found out and told my parents. All hell broke loose. My dad was so angry. One night, John and I were sitting in his car outside my house, as I had told him my family knew about him, and suddenly my sister Jane started banging on the window and telling him to f-off. Well, we drove off, as we liked to park down quiet lanes and just talk, kiss and…nothing else, lol! God, I was just too scared to have sex. It got to a point where I felt the relationship wasn't going anywhere. I knew my parents wouldn't accept John because of his age, so I ended it. Boy, what fun experience, though. I was kinda realising I could find guys of all ages.

Before going to the pub, me and the girls would go to the off licence, buy some alcohol and have a good drink. My mum said to me, "I hope you don't ever go down Shaky-Jakes." Now, you are all probably wondering what this was. Well, it was a place that my elder brother Bill used to go to – a field near to a school called St Chads. Bill and his friends used to meet on this field and light a bonfire. Bill played his guitar and many hippy-like people and rockers would turn up to drink, smoke and have a sing around the bonfire. They named the field Shaky-

Jakes. Well, when my mum said she hoped I didn't go there, the first thing I did was to get all my friends together and head straight over.

I had a little drink and was raring to see what was going on there. We could see the big bonfire and could hear loads of people laughing, singing and playing around. I saw Bill playing his guitar and OMG, there were loads of people. It was quite exciting. Bill seemed shocked that I had turned up with my mates. "Do Mum and Dad know you're down here?" he asked. "Yeah, of course," I replied. There were bikers there, too, and oh, they looked so good with their leathers and long hair. My friends and I were quite enjoying being there. The next thing I knew, a few guys turned up and whooohooo, they looked quite cool. They were what we would call smoothies. As they stood around the bomby, they drank bottles of old English cider. Many, of course, were smoking the old wacky baccy too. I couldn't stop looking at one of the guys – he was so gawjuss and had the most beautiful blue eyes. Anyway, I asked my bro who he was and he told me his name was Wayne Masters. Me and my mates quite enjoyed being down Shaky-Jakes, especially now there were some lush-looking guys going down there, too. Well, one lush-looking guy. As the fire burned, Wayne started looking over, so I looked back. My heart was beating quite excitedly and I was saying to my mates, "I think he's just the guy for me." Well, my brother's friend, Paul Henry (God bless him, he's passed to heaven now) was very much a hippy and he had long black hair. He was one of my brother's close mates from childhood. Anyway, he said about us all going back to his house for a party. Even better, as we were walking down the alley, Wayne was behind me. "What's your name, then?"

he asked. I couldn't believe he had actually spoken to me. So, of course, I replied – it would be rude not to, aye? Anyway, we all went back to Paul's and the party began. I don't think my brother really wanted me there, as there was a lot of the wacky baccy going round, but I wasn't really bothered by that – I just wanted to talk with Wayne. We finally got chatting and he asked where I came from. I said I was Bill's sister. Nothing much happened that night and we left about 3am. Before dropping my friends home, we arranged to go back there the following night.

The birds were singing as I drove home on my own. I felt excited about going to Shaky-Jakes again. I hoped that Wayne would be there too. I was dreading going home, as I knew Mum and Dad would be up waiting for me. We weren't seeing eye-to-eye still because I was changing so much, even more so since learning to drive. For once I felt free and independent. I was like any 'normal' person. It was great just knowing that if I wanted to go out I could, and on my own. It's very hard to explain to you, the reader, how I've felt at times, having to rely on my family to help me in so many ways. Just imagine how all through my life I've tried to be independent and to do things like dress, wash my body and hair, and even brush my teeth, without help. Most importantly, I've always taken myself to the toilet. But sometimes there were days when I needed a little help – more so if I was out and having to use a public toilet. I would need some help if I wore clothing that was difficult and would have to go into the loo with my mum or sisters. That wasn't always comfortable for me, especially if there were others waiting. As I got older and became a bit cheeky, I would say, "Don't worry, guys, we're lesbians." How my mum would tut, lol. Having my car meant I didn't need to ask my dad to take me places anymore. Plus, sometimes, just to annoy Mum, I would go out, have a drink and then pop back in to let her know I was drinking and wouldn't be coming home until whatever time. She would tell me off and we would argue. In the end, I'd storm out. When I think about all this now, I feel quite ashamed of myself for putting my parents through all that worry every night by going out and them knowing I would have a drink. But I guess I needed to prove to both of them that I was living a 'normal' life. I was having fun and wanted to be in control, but how worrying for them. I'd hide my keys so they wouldn't find them, as I would have hated for them to take them away. My car had become my pride and joy. Before getting it, I often worried that I wouldn't be able to drive, or that I would be offered one of the three-wheeler, blue disabled cars, which were just awful. I always used to say I would never, ever be seen in one of them.

I had become so independent. I had done everything for myself apart from cooking – Mum never let me in the kitchen. My brother told my parents about me venturing to Shaky-Jakes and my mum asked why I wanted to go down there. She also asked if Donna's dad knew what we were up to. I just replied, "None of your business," and carried on doing what I wanted.

Again, I felt I was in control by annoying my parents. It makes me so sad to write this. They gave me so much help and taught me right from wrong, yet they now had an uncontrollable daughter. OMG, how could I have put them through this? Sorry Mum and Dad, but I guess I needed to prove to this crazy, mucked-up world that I could and would be 'normal'.

Anyway, I made sure all my friends were up for another night down Shaky-Jakes. But the trouble with getting in late nearly every night was that I didn't want to go to work at Bisons in the morning, and I started skipping days. I would do maybe two or three days a week in total. In the end, the guy who was in charge when the main boss John wasn't in – a guy called Peter, I always thought he was a total drip and I didn't really like him – called me into his office and asked if I really wanted this job. Well, I know now my attitude stunk, but I said I wasn't really enjoying the work and I didn't want to do it anymore. Then I left. I think I let my dad down, as he had got me the job. But most of my friends weren't working and all I could think about was fun, fun, fun.

On Saturday nights, me and my mates would get a Chinese takeaway and eat it up in my bedroom. Then we'd go out, either to Shaky-Jakes or the Greyhound pub, where my cousin Kenny and his friends used to go. On one particular night, we were out and I had to pop home for something. As I pulled up outside our house, I saw my dad standing at our gate. "Oh dear, what have I done?" I said to my mates. I unwound my window and said, "What's up, Dad?" He looked worried, asked where I'd been and then told me to go in. My friends remained silent in the car as I said, "God, what now?" I thought it was about me being out all day. Anyway, when I got in, Dad said that Donna needed to go home. "But we are about to go out," I protested. Dad repeated in his angry voice that she needed to go home NOW. Well, when he told me why, OMG. Donna's mum had died while doing her shopping. She had suffered a heart attack in the car park. I was devastated and went back to the car, where Donna, Tracey and my mate Sue were waiting for me. "Did you get a telling off?" they asked. "Are we going for a Chinese now?" My heart was feeling so, so sad. I just said, "No, Don, you gotta go home, mate." Then I started driving. Donna asked why, but I just couldn't say anything, as my dad had said that Donna's auntie would be waiting for her when she got home. Well, as I pulled up, her Aunt Jess was at the front door. "OMG, something must be up," Donna said. When Donna got out of the car, I started to cry. My other friends said, "What's wrong?" So I told them and then took them home. It was so, so sad for her, after all she was my best mate. Her mum Alice was a wonderful lady. Once, I was arranging a birthday party, so I went round to Donna's house to invite her mum and dad. Alice used to call me 'Queen Bee' and as it was a hot day, she asked if I would like some ice cream. "No thank you," I replied. "Go on," Alice urged. "I won't look." She knew I didn't like to eat outside my home, and that made me laugh. You see, I had started feeling self-conscious about using my feet outside my comfort zone. So, to Alice Netting, I send my love to you in heaven.

CHAPTER TWELVE

Meeting My Husband To Be

Well, to be told from a young age that I would probably never marry was awful. OMG, I'm glad my parents kept me, loved me and showed me how to live a normal life. I knew from seeing Wayne that first night down Shaky-Jakes that he was the man for me. When we finally got to really know each other, I was sure we were meant to be together, but it wasn't easy at first, as a few people didn't think we were right for each other, including other family members. Many worried that Wayne was only around me for my money. OMG, how ridiculous. My trust money was only for me, so there was no way that even if he did want me for my money, he would have got his hands on it. When we heard people talking about this, I urged Wayne not to let it bother him. But one particular night it must have got to him and he told me we needed to end our friendship. I was devastated and when I found out that certain family members had suggested our break-up, I became so angry. Wayne didn't want me for my money at all, but we were now over anyway. I went out with my mates and got absolutely drunk. First, I went round to Sue's house with Donna and Tracey and hit the gin and bitter lemon. Then we went to the Greyhound pub, which my lovely cousin Kenny used to frequent. He was always there at the corner of the bar with his mates. One of them was Andy, who had been the best man at my sister Sue's wedding. I was 14 when she got married and I was chief bridesmaid. I actually had a bit of a crush on Andy, whom everyone called Dicko, lol. Well, many a time before I was seeing Wayne I used to go out and about with Kenny and Andy. My friend Sue had a big crush on Kenny.

While Andy and me had become friends, I knew he wasn't for me, although one time he did say he would make a good husband. But no, I didn't feel any chemistry. However, his interest proved that as I got older, I was feeling more attractive and confident. I did like to tease. Oh yes, naughty but nice, lol. Also, my parents knew Dicko. Um, could it be that they wanted us to be more than just friends? I wanted guys who were a bit more exciting and didn't know my family. I think that's why I used to travel to Liverpool at weekends. No one knew me there apart from my friend Mandy Hendrie.

So, back to the night at the Greyhound. There I was rolling drunk. God knows how I drove there. I was being so, so bad, but stubborn me was doing what I wanted. I told Kenny about how I'd been dumped and how my family had put their boot in. And to think that a very GAWJUSS, good-looking guy fancied me, but that it had all be ruined by others poking their noses into my life. I was pretty angry. If only they knew that the big fear in my life was that nobody would ever want me. Now I'd finally found a guy that I felt comfortable with, and some people were trying to destroy it.

Well, I decided to go back to Jersey to get away from feeling sad about being dumped. Jane came with me and I also took a photo of Wayne. For the entire two weeks I was away I just couldn't get him out my head, I so wanted to get him back. Anyway, after the holiday, I was driving down Tilbury hoping to bump into Wayne, when, OMG, who should be walking home? I couldn't believe it. I pulled over and he said he hadn't seen me around. I told him I had been away. I asked if he fancied going for a drink and he actually said yes, so we decided to take a ride to Canvey Island, which is another little town near us. I just wanted to be away from our town. We had a good long talk and I told him I never, ever believed he was with me for my money. From that day on, we started seeing each other again. I finally knew that Wayne was the one for me. Our relationship grew even stronger.

And, my dear readers, Wayne was the one who took my virginity. Yep, I had waited a long time to find a special guy who'd make me feel good and safe, and, most importantly, who I'd want to lose my virginity to. I never wanted to sleep around. Oh no, definitely not. I wanted it to be with the right guy and yep, Wayne was definitely that person. I also knew I wanted his babies. My dream was to have two daughters. I did tell Wayne a little white lie and made out I was on the pill when nope, I definitely wasn't. That was very naughty, I know, but he was so bloody gawjuss and he had the most beautiful blue eyes ever.

Well, before long, I found out I was pregnant! It was odd really, coz my younger sister Jane, who was 16, had recently shocked my parents by announcing she was having a baby. Then came my news. OMG, my poor parents! I remember Mum coming to the doctor's with me to have the pregnancy confirmed. "How will we tell Dad?" I asked. Well, he was preparing our dinner one evening when he asked if everything was OK. I looked at my mum and she said, "Not really, Mandy's pregnant." All Dad said was, "Well, is he gonna marry you, then?" I said that Wayne didn't know my news yet. There were five months between my sister's pregnancy and mine, and my parents were only just coming to terms with Jane's news. Well, that night, me and Wayne went for a drive and parked up at a place called Coalhouse Fort. I told him the news. Well, he went quiet at first and I really thought he was going to dump me again. "What did your parents say?" he asked. I laughed and told him what my dad had said. Wayne laughed too and said, "Well, I will marry you if you want, but I've now got to tell my parents." And he didn't just have to explain about the pregnancy. At that point, his parents didn't even know he was seeing anyone, let alone someone with no arms. The news didn't take long to get out. What we didn't know was that one of Wayne's mates from St Chad's Social Club had opened his mouth to Wayne's dad and told him about me and the pregnancy. So his parents did know. I guess they were just waiting for Wayne to tell them. I think they were concerned that their son was about to get involved with a girl with no arms. They didn't know me, remember, and his mum was especially worried. When he told them she did ask him how I would do his cooking and things, bless her.

At this stage of my life, I forgot about my seabed and visualised a cake instead. Yep, I started my first cake with the base, which was very solid, and every time I achieved something that the doctors, way back when I was born, had said would be impossible, I made another layer, until my cake had many tiers. Now, when my cake was finally finished, I needed to put a cherry on the top. This cherry was my first grandchild. Yep, I'd led a normal life, found a man who loved me, had two beautiful daughters and now I was a grandmother to Callum. Wow, just wow.

Anyway, once Wayne's parents came to terms with me having no arms, they then had to come to terms with the fact I was having his baby. I remember the first time I met them. I was really nervous and I wouldn't have a drink, not even a cup of tea. I guess I didn't want to use my feet in front of them. Even as time went on, I never really used my feet in their company.

So, once everyone knew I was pregnant, it was time to start arranging our wedding, as I wanted to tie the knot before the baby arrived. I remember talking to my sister Sue and she said, "Why don't you have a winter wedding?" So, we booked our big day for 19th December 1981. Going to look for my wedding and bridesmaid dresses was so exciting. I had to pick out my pageboy outfit too. I wanted loads of bridesmaids and ended up having my little nieces, Shiree, Samantha and Julie. I chose my nephew Lee to be my pageboy. My sister Sue and my friends Donna and Sandra were also bridesmaids. My sister-in-law, another Sue, stepped in for Jane, who by then was heavily pregnant.

The special day had arrived. The odd thing was, though, the night before it had snowed heavily and I was worried that my dress would get ruined. The next morning, when I woke up, the snow had completely disappeared. How odd, aye?

The morning was very busy, as my bridesmaids and I went off to the hairdressers. There were so many people in and out of my house – phew, what a morning. Then it was time to get into my beautiful wedding dress. My mum and Jane helped and boy, was my heart beating excitably. I was ready, oh yes, all dressed and ready to go downstairs. I will always remember how my darling cousin Kenny was waiting at the bottom of our stairs. He looked up at me with his lovely, bright blue eyes and said, "You look beautiful, Mand." Ah, bless him. I so miss our Ken, as he passed to heaven many years later. I will always love you, Kenny Hornsby. You were my number one cousin and a good friend, too. Well, I went into our living room to have photos taken and my handsome nephew Lee held my dress so I didn't trip. He was a wonderful pageboy and looked very smart in his suit. I can't believe that he too is no longer with us. It makes me so sad to type this, knowing that Lee went to heaven at 16 after being murdered.

Anyway, it was time to go, and me and my very smart dad got into the white Rolls Royce and off we drove to the church, which was in Chadwell St Mary, Thurrock. Along the way, I can remember seeing people who knew me at the shops, and they waved and smiled at me. I felt so excited, but in my mind I was thinking, *OMG, I'm marrying the most gawjuss, handsome guy, whom I never thought I would ever meet, and I'm dressed in my gawjuss wedding dress and there's a baby in my tummy.* What an amazing feeling going through my body. The only thing missing is that I would have loved to be able to hold my dad's arm when we walked down the aisle to the altar. I must admit I felt a bit sad when we got out of the beautiful car and stood at the church door waiting for the music to begin.

The church doors opened and the vicar asked all the bridesmaids and my pageboy to get into their places. Then the church organist started playing and in we went. OMG, everyone was looking at me, and there was Wayne with my brother Kevin as his best man – Wayne's mate had let him down by drinking far too much the previous night, which had led to my bro stepping in. Anyway, Wayne and I were so nervous and we were worried that we wouldn't get the words out right. But yep, it all went fantastically well. Wayne was worried that as he went to put the gold chain around my neck with my wedding ring on it, he would be far too shaky to tie the little clasp, but he did so well. Once again, I wished I had hands so I'd be able to put Wayne's wedding ring on his finger, but bless him, he put it on himself. So, we were husband and wife at last. After the service we had an amazing sit-down meal and then danced the night away. We didn't go on honeymoon, though, we just went to our new home and enjoyed living together as Mr and Mrs Masters. Every time I conquered things in my journey of life, I made a cake in my mind, adding tiers when things felt good and right. It was really like a wedding cake, I guess, but I knew the day would come when I would place a bright red cherry on top of the cake. Then I'd know that I'd made it through life. The cherry wasn't there yet, so I knew I had more to do.

CHAPTER THIRTEEN

Motherhood

Every day during my first five months of pregnancy, I had very bad sickness and lost weight. After that it calmed down, thank God. I remember going to my antenatal appointments. Jane was further ahead than me, but sometimes we went together. I hated going and for some reason I didn't really like being in the waiting room with other expectant mothers. I'm not sure why. At least I knew the midwife. When I first met her she said to me, "OMG, it's Mandy Hornsby, isn't it!" I replied, "Yes, but now I'm Mandy Masters." She said she remembered my birth at Orsett Hopsital in Grays. She told me how she used to look after my dear mum, and she could remember holding me, too. "I've often wondered how you were getting on," she said. I was pleased to have her, as she spoiled me rotten from that day on and made me feel so at ease. I must admit that when I was pregnant I never, ever worried that our baby might be born without any arms. I do remember the consultant asking to see me one day, as he was worried about me giving birth normally. When I asked why, he replied that I might not have a normal pelvis. Plus, I wouldn't be able to hold my legs up while giving birth.

What? OMG.

I told the consultant that in no way did I want a C-section, as I wouldn't be able to hold our baby in my legs. I also planned to breastfeed, and having a big cut across my belly wasn't something I could think about. The consultant said I would need to have an X-ray and have my pelvis measured. I went home and cried. Mum was angry with the consultant and said she would come with me the next time I went. Well, the appointment came and I had to stand with my legs apart while the woman measured in between them. After that I had a few X-rays. We were then told to wait in the waiting room until the consultant had seen my results. My insides were anxious and my mind was angry, but I had my hubby beside me as well as a very determined mum. Anyway, we were called in and my mum straight away told the doctor that I would be quite capable of giving birth normally. She explained to him how all through my life I had done everything normally, and she said how ridiculous it was for him to say I wouldn't be able to hold my own legs up. "The thing with Mandy is that she will always find a way, her way, and deal with it." So, when the results came through that my pelvis was OK to give birth, the consultant agreed, thank God.

As my tummy got bigger, I struggled a bit to use my feet, but I still loved being pregnant. Well, the day arrived and I went into labour on the 14th May 1982. The labour seemed to last forever – boy was that one long evening. I couldn't believe it when a nurse came in and said, "Mrs Masters, I have to shave you now." I asked, "Shave me where?" Lol, she explained that the area where the baby was going to come out from had to be shaved. Oh, OK, but I defiantly wasn't happy about having it done. But then she said that wasn't all.

What?!

She explained that she was going to give me an enema so that my bowels would be empty. OMG, I couldn't believe that within minutes of this being inserted, I was sitting on the loo. Let me tell you, I was not a happy bunny. I was so scared and my labour went on for a long time. They eventually decided to break my waters. I can remember the midwife coming into the room with what looked like a massive and long knitting needle. OMG, what was she going to do? She explained how she was going to break my waters with it. Talk about being even more scared, but Wayne was with me all the way. Well, once my waters had been broken, the pain started even worse than before. Wayne was given gas and air to hold, and I was told that I was to use it when the pain became unbearable. Well, I used it alright. I think I used it well. Wow, I loved the feeling of the gas and air, lol. Well, I had to push and push and I cried and cried. First of all they put my legs up in slings, but I was so uncomfortable that I asked them to take them away and let me do it my way. They agreed and after a long labour and much pain, our baby girl was born. I kept asking, "Is it a girl? Is it a girl?" I had always wanted a girl. Before meeting Wayne, I had my tarot cards read in Canvey Island, and the lady predicted I would meet him. She got his name right and even where we would meet. When I fell pregnant, I went back to see her and told her how right she'd been. She told me I was going to have a baby boy, and that it could be twins. Well, I felt sad, as I'd only ever wanted two daughters. So, throughout my pregnancy, I just kept thinking, *"Oh, a boy."* When Wayne said, "It's a girl!" I cried, "Oh my God, Oh my God." They laid our little girl on my chest. Wayne and I had a little cry and then I remember a doctor being called in, as the midwife had noticed I was bleeding a lot. They asked Wayne to wait outside while they laid our baby girl in the little glass crib. I remember looking at her and thinking, *You're gonna be called Nicola Louise.* The doctor examined me and noticed that my bottom area had a tear and needed stitching. So, as our little girl was laying in her little crib making baby noises, Mummy was having her bottom area stitched. I remember that the very young man who came to stitch me up had bright ginger hair, and all I can remember is thinking, *OMG, how young are you!*

I'd always said that I wanted to breastfeed, but the nurses weren't sure how I was going to do it. First of all, they asked if I wanted my mattress put on the floor. I just laughed and asked them why. Well, they thought it would be easier for me to be on the floor. I asked them to let me do things my way. I used to wake early with Nicola, get her out of her crib and have her all dressed before the nurses came in. Back in those days, babies wore little nightdresses and the nurses couldn't believe I had dressed Nicola and tied the tiny bows at the back. I think everyone was either shocked or gobsmacked when I cradled Nicola in my legs and placed my boob in her mouth to feed. I didn't want a fuss, I just wanted to get home and start our lives like a normal family. The hospital staff wanted me to do a video to show mothers who complained that they couldn't do this or that and moaned all the time. They wanted to show how I had coped giving birth and looking after our baby. I said no, but thinking back, I guess I should have said yes. The day arrived to take my baby girl home. I was so excited and couldn't wait for Wayne to come and get us. It was nerve wracking really, as it was now just Wayne and me and our baby girl. Also, having stitches was very uncomfortable, especially when I used my feet. I'd helped look after my siblings' children, so I wasn't worried that I couldn't do things that other mums could do, such as change nappies. A few weeks after arriving home, I did feel quite tearful. Wayne was asleep on the sofa and I was holding Nicola, when I started to think, *Oh, what if I can't cope and poor Wayne's left to do everything?* The tears started flowing down my face. Wayne woke up and couldn't believe I was crying. This lasted just a few days and the doctor explained that sometimes women experience post-natal depression after giving birth. Urgh, no way did I want that! After a few days I was fine. I could only breastfeed Nicola for about two months, as I developed milk fever. Boy, was that horrible. Nicola was a very good little girl and I always used terry-towelling nappies to change her bum. My friends were amazed that I could put the big pin in. May I say that I never, ever pricked my baby girl or my tootsies, lol. Because my brothers and sisters had let me help with their babies, even down to bathing them, I was never nervous of giving Nicola a bath. I used to get Wayne to place her head on my right foot and I would wash her with my left one. Though I did always get Wayne to wash her hair.

CHAPTER FOURTEEN

Adding To Our Brood

My mum and Jane often came round to help out. I think it was also to give Wayne a little break. He wasn't working, which was good timing as he could help take care of Nicola. She was about one when we started talking about him going back.

Nicola was quite a mature little girl and when Wayne went back to work when she was two, it was lovely having some mummy time with her. She had the most beautiful eyes and I used to get all my make up out and put it on her. She loved putting lipstick on by herself. I remember watching her looking in the mirror and pouting and posing, bless her. Then she would ask me to paint and decorate her beautiful fingernails. I remember going into a jewellery shop one day and the lady saw Nicola's hands and said, "Oh, what beautiful, sparkly nails." She asked me who'd done them and I replied, "I did them with me tootsies." Well, she looked at me with amazement and said, "Gosh, you do better with your toes than I could do with my hands." I guess people just can't picture that toes can sometimes be better than fingers. Well, my toes are, lol!

When Nicola was three, she started playschool. I wanted another baby and had suffered a few miscarriages. I started to wonder if I was ever going to have another little one. I can remember going to see my doctor and telling him I was worried something was wrong. He explained that as I had put on a bit of weight since having Nicola, falling pregnant might be harder. I had noticed that my weight had started to change, but I couldn't seem to shift the extra pounds. I tried dieting and even went to see a private doctor, who gave me some slimming pills. I soon came off them because they made me feel quite unwell. I wasn't in the right mood to diet and just thought, *Oh well, at least I have one child.* We were so happy on the day I found out I was pregnant again. I did say to Wayne that when we had a new baby, I wanted to do most of the care. When Nicola was born, Wayne was there to help, but now he was building petrol stations and at times he had to travel quite far away.

The only struggle this time was getting my blood, as I had put on a lot of weight. When pregnant with Nicola, the nurses had taken blood from my neck. Boy, did that hurt. So, they asked me to spend an afternoon on a ward. They tilted my bed back so that all the blood would run straight to my head. OMG, I hated it, but I knew it had to be done. It worked and made the veins in my neck come out a bit.

I was overdue again, just like with Nicola, so they said they wanted to induce me. Off we went to Orsett Hospital. They got me settled and I can remember that *EastEnders* was just about to start as my mum and dad were leaving to go home. "Oh, I'm starting to get niggling pains," I said. The nurse told me to have a warm bath and see what happened. So, Wayne sat with me while I had a soak. The pains started to get worse, so the nurse checked me and said I had a little while to go yet. I can remember lying on my bed and the pain becoming stronger. They brought me some gas and air and the nurse told me that they had fitted something on the end of the gas tube, which I could bite instead of having to use the mask. She looked at Wayne and told him to give me the gas and air when the pain got worse. Well, once I got used to the gas, I wanted more and more, lol. I felt like pushing and Wayne called the nurse in. "Not yet, Mandy," she said. "Your waters haven't broken yet." With that, I suddenly thought I had wet the bed. When I told the nurse she explained that my waters had gone and she urged me not to push just yet. She wanted to take me to another room. Well, she popped out and hadn't been gone five minutes when I said to Wayne, "I think the baby's coming." He started to panic and called for the nurse. She examined me and said, "Not quite yet," and then added, "I think we will get you to walk to the other room."

Walk? Whaaat?

I wondered if she was having a laugh. I could feel the baby's head, but the nurse insisted it wasn't there yet. As I struggled getting onto the bed in the other room, the nurse said, "I will be back in a mo, Mandy." As I lay there, I felt I had to push. Then Wayne started to panic – he had seen our baby's head. He shouted out for the nurse. I was on a lot of gas and air and hated the pain. The nurse couldn't believe how quickly I had dilated. I said, "I told you the head was there." Well, I had another urge to push, but this time it was a very big push, and out came our baby. "Is it a girl, Wayne? Is it a girl?" That's all I kept asking, as I was quite high on the gas and air. "Yes, it's a girl!" OMG, I was so relieved when the nurse placed our new baby girl on my chest and she started to cry. "Let's weigh her now," the nurse suggested. It turned out that my brand new daughter was 8lb exactly. Her name is Marie Joanne. Jane had called her second daughter Joanne Marie, and we thought it would be nice to reverse her name. I couldn't believe I didn't need any stitches this time. The hospital allowed us to bring our pram in, so we didn't have to put Marie in one of those horrible glass tanks.

Well, the next morning, I started breastfeeding. The nurses were amazed at how well I coped. Wayne brought Nicola over after playschool and I couldn't wait for her to meet her baby sister. She came running in with gifts and a beaming smile, and she wanted to hold Marie straight away. I knew then that our family was complete. I had only ever wanted two girls – for some reason I didn't want boys. If Wayne wanted one, he never said. This time I was determined not to get that horrible post-natal depression I'd had for a short while after giving birth to Nicola.

When changing Marie, I used disposable nappies. OMG, it was so much easier – no more bloody pins, lol. As time went on and Nicola reached school age, I was a bit worried about the other children finding out that her mummy didn't have any arms. I remember that Nicola was so excited about her first day. When we took her into class, some little girls came over and asked her if she wanted to play with them. I couldn't believe it – they hadn't even noticed that I didn't have any arms. Maybe it was because as an adult, I didn't wear short sleeves, as I had when I was younger, and I didn't feel so self-conscious. I always wore long sleeves, but I never tucked them in as my mum used to do. I hated that. Nicola's first day was a success and she seemed really happy. I was bathing Nicola one day, when I asked her, "Do your friends know Mummy doesn't have any arms?" Nicola replied sweetly, "No, I didn't tell them, as I wouldn't want you to cry." Ahh, bless. "Mummy doesn't mind, darling," I said. "You can tell them." Then one day after school, Nicola asked if her friend Rachel could come round to play. "Maybe tomorrow," I said. Well, she was so excited and asked me to tell Rachel's mum. I duly spoke to her and said, "I don't know if your Rachel knows that I haven't got any arms, but will she be OK?" Her mum reassured me that she'd been fine and that she did know about my situation. She explained, "She came home one day and told me that Nicola's mummy hasn't got any arms and uses her feet instead." So, I guess Nicola had started telling her school friends. Well, the day came for Rachel to come home with us. When she got into my car she was amazed how I could drive. She thought my car must be magic because the steering wheel went round on its own, lol. Anyway, they played so nicely and then asked if they could have some yogurt. I can remember Rachel saying, "Do you want me to undo the carton as you don't have any hands?" Well, I laughed and my Nicola said, "My mummy can undo it, silly. She uses her feet." And from that day on, Nicola had many little friends round to play. I think I worried over nothing.

Anyway, when Marie was around two, I decided I would put her in some baby reins. I extended the handle using a bag handle, which I then placed around my neck before putting the reins on Marie. I thought it would be nice to take her for a little walk up the road near the Haven, where all the old-age pensioners lived. There was a little grassy area nearby, which I used to play on when I was little. Well, oh my giddy

God, as soon as we walked onto the grass, Marie screamed. She hadn't really walked on grass before, as Wayne had patioed our garden. Well, she wouldn't walk and just kept crying. So I thought, *Well, I can't carry her, but I can get my teeth around the harness.* So, I bloody well carried her home in my mouth, lol. Thank God we weren't far away from the house. I had to laugh, as it reminded me of a bitch carrying her puppies in her mouth. But at least we got home. Phew, never, ever again, lol. It's funny thinking back now. Whenever I went out with my girls they never ran off. And when we went shopping they held my sleeve. They seemed to know that they shouldn't wander off. People used to say, "Aren't your girls good!" And yes, I'm proud to say that they were the best. I never, ever wanted them to grow up having to look after Mummy. I wanted them to be normal little girls and didn't want them doing anything. In reality, I made a rod for my own back, as when they got to about 10, I would say, "Isn't it about time you started making your own beds?" I also asked them to empty the dishwasher from time to time, and boy did they moan.

I loved putting their hair up, either in a ponytail or bunches, and peeps were amazed I could do it with my toes. All I wanted was to be was a housewife and an independent mum. I loved being a mummy and I was lucky to have the most understanding and helpful hubby, too.

When Marie was about seven months old, I fell pregnant again. I was so shocked. I can remember going to the chemist with my Sue and a water sample. We were told to come back in about an hour to see if I was pregnant. Anyway, Sue went into the chemist while I waited in the car with Marie. OMG, positive! "No way, I don't believe you," I said. So Sue went back into the chemist and then the guy in there came out and said, "Yes, Mandy, it's positive." I was upset, as I really wasn't ready for another baby. I went to see my doctor and he said, "Mandy, you don't have to go ahead with this pregnancy. You can have a termination." Sue was with me and I felt so confused, as I didn't believe in abortion. I told the doctor I would think about it. I'd been busy arranging a surprise birthday party for Wayne and I said to my sis that I would decide about the baby once it was over. I didn't tell anyone, but by Sunday morning I had lost some clumps of blood. I went to my doctor and he said I may have had a miscarriage. He sent me over to the hospital for a scan. Sue came with me and it was confirmed that the baby was gone. I guess baby number three wasn't to be.

Anyway, when Marie was about three years old, I can remember feeling very unwell. I hadn't had a period for two months, so I went to get a pregnancy test carried out, which came back negative. I thought nothing of it until I skipped my next period. So I went to see my doctor and he said, "Let's see if you have a period next month." Well, nothing again. I still felt really unwell so Wayne called the doctor in, as I was in a lot of pain. He felt my tummy and asked if I had opened my bowels at all. I said I was having problems going, so he gave me some tablets for constipation. I took them for a few days and can remember what happened next as if it was yesterday. It was a Saturday and my dad phoned and asked if Wayne fancied going fishing. I was bleeding heavily and Wayne said he wouldn't go, as I was obviously not feeling too well. My mum said she would come and sit with me for the day, so that Wayne could enjoy his fishing trip. I was lying on the sofa chatting away with Mum, when I felt I needed a wee. Well, just as I got into the toilet, a gush of water came out and I felt a large lump of stuff come away from me. I screamed out for Mum and she came into the loo and pulled my knickers down. OMG, there was a large bag that resembled a brain. I was crying and Mum tried to calm me down. She called for my doctor and he was already there by the time Wayne and my dad walked through the door. Mum told them what had happened. The doctor asked to see what I had lost and my mum brought out this thing on a saucer. The doctor looked at it and I explained how I thought I'd peed myself, as this gush of water came out, followed by the lump. He looked at me and said, "Mandy, I'm so sorry but this is the bag that a baby grows in. The water that you lost first was the water breaking." I was in shock and crying so much that the doctor called Wayne in to try and calm me down. All I could think about was how there must have been a tiny baby in that bag. I made the doctor look and he said there was nothing. However, I didn't believe him, so I made Wayne look too, which must have been awful for him. I asked the doctor why all the tests had come back negative. I was fuming, especially as I'd taken those stupid constipation tablets, too. The doctor apologised and said I didn't need a D&C, as everything had come away. Then he left. Well, my mum and dad stayed for a while and Nicola and Marie went to sleep at my sister's for the night, as I just cried and cried and cried. I wouldn't let Wayne throw the fleshy bag away. No, I made him put it in a paper bag. I know that sounds disgusting, and Wayne wasn't happy about having it sitting in this paper bag on a saucer, but I still felt there could be a baby in there. Yes, I know the doctor and Wayne had looked in it, but I needed to look myself. When I felt ready, I did just that. It definitely looked like a brain, with veins in it and a hole. I prodded it with a pen and managed to open the hole. Yep, it was empty. There was definitely no baby, but in my mind I needed to make sure. God knows, if there had been a tiny baby I think I would have been a wreck. Anyway, I was now ready for Wayne to throw it away. The next day, my sisters Jane and Sue came round along with my friend Donna. I had chocolates and flowers brought for me, but no one really knew what to say. It was the most horrible feeling ever and I was so angry with my doctor. But I also realised that I had only ever wanted two daughters, which we'd already been blessed with, and I felt very happy with my little family. My life felt complete. If only those doctors could have seen me. You know, the ones who had wanted my mum and dad to think about putting me in a home and didn't think I'd live past 19. The ones who said I'd need a lot of caring for and probably wouldn't have any children. Well, I've always said that if I had hands, I would stick two fingers up at them stupid doctors and say, "No one stops me, I'm a survivor of thalidomide!"

CHAPTER FIFTEEN

The Cherry On The Cake

Well, finally all my dreams had come true. Yep, I'd found my gawjuss hubby Wayne and had my two beautiful daughters, Nicola and Marie. I never wanted my daughters to do a thing for me, as I wanted to be like any other mummy and bring them up living a normal life. I also wanted to do everything a wife could possibly do, from cleaning the house to preparing dinner. I was never a good cook, though. My mum wouldn't let me in the kitchen as a child, and I wasn't really into cooking when I was younger.

Bringing my girls up wasn't hard at all, as they were both quick learners and seemed to know that Mummy couldn't pick them up like Daddy could. When I took them out, people used to remark how good they were by staying by my side and holding my long sleeves. I always made sure that when they went to playschool and big school it was me that put their hair up –Wayne didn't have a clue, lol. The only style I could never do was the French plait, but I did ponytails and plaiting. The French plait was a bit too fiddly, which was frustrating, as I was determined to do everything my way.

I used to worry about my girls getting mocked at their schools, but I gave talks about my situation and all the children accepted it. At times, I thought about my dear mum and wondered if she ever worried about me being bullied at school. But to be honest, I think I was too strong-minded and a bit of a bossy boots, too. I wanted to be the leader of many things. I'm glad I wasn't treated any different to my five siblings, and I'm glad I was brought up to never say, "I can't." Mum always used to say, "There's no such word." She never hid me away from anyone, and I guess she was determined to make me stronger and no different from any of her other children.

I loved being a wife to Wayne and a mum to my girls. It's all I ever wanted. I needed to prove something, not only to those depressing doctors who judged me when I was born, but also to the others who looked in on my life and probably thought, *How's she gonna cope?* But I bloody did!

I learnt to cook, and may I say very well, too. When Wayne started work, I didn't want him coming home and having to make dinner for us all. I loved cooking and dishing out the dinners. I can remember our friends, Pam and Steve, popping in one Sunday. I was in the middle of doing a Sunday roast and was sitting on my stool, using my feet to move a dish from the kitchen unit to the oven. So, so easy. Pam had every faith in me and didn't blink an eye, but Steve, bless him, said, "You don't lift that out when it's hot, do you?" I laughed and said, "Yes, Steve." Lol. I suppose he just couldn't imagine that feet can actually do this, but hey hoo, they can!

I also loved making and icing birthday cakes. I was very good at making dolls with big fancy crinoline dresses. Again, I taught myself and before long friends and family were asking me to make them a cake. My talents just got stronger. I would always hear my mum saying, "Never say you can't", and that made me do things my way, but better. Actually, thinking about it, I think I can do many things better than people who do have hands.

However, my cherry on the cake was when my daughters gave me grandchildren. Instead of having my seabed, I visualised a tiered cake. Yep, as I achieved things, such as becoming a wife and mother, I'd make a cake in my mind. And, as more achievements were ticked off my list, my cake started to resemble a wedding cake, with several tiers. But I knew my cake wouldn't be complete without a big, glossy cherry on the top. Well, the day came when my Nicola fell pregnant. Now, let me tell you something. When I was around 16, I had a love of tarot card readings. My mum and my aunt Joan used to see a few people. Well, they were booked in to see a Mrs Clack from Canvey Island in Essex. I asked if I could go with them. Mrs Clack did our readings from her small kitchen. Well, my time arrived and gosh, I was excited. She actually told me I would meet my husband in a strange place, and she even said that his name would be Wayne. Wow! At the time I didn't know anyone called Wayne. I asked her if I would have children and she said two boys, maybe twins. Ummm, I was a twin, but Mum lost my sibling at an early stage in the pregnancy.

Anyway, I felt a little disappointed, as I'd only ever wanted two girls. As time went on, most of Mrs Clack's predictions came true. I did meet a Wayne and it was definitely in a strange place, but I ended up with two girls rather than twin boys. Anyway, I went on to have quite a few more readings and I can remember one tarot reader asking, "Do you have a daughter?"

I replied, "Yes, two." Then she said the older one, my Nicola, who was then about 10, would bring me a shock when she got to the age of around 15. "Shock? In what way?" I asked. The tarot reader looked at me and said, "Well, all I can say is that you'll cry for a whole day." I asked why and felt worried, so the lady reassured me it was nothing serious, but she refused to tell me anything else. Bloody hell, I was a bit angry, as having that reading had left me hanging. Anyway, getting to the cherry, lol, when Nicola got to 15, the shock did hit us. I had noticed that she wasn't having her periods. I must admit that she had come to ask me if she could go on the pill, as she was seeing a young lad. I replied that I would ask her dad. But when I raised it, Wayne just said no and that he didn't want to talk about it. The next day, I told Nic what her dad had said and reassured her that I would take her to the doctors when she was 16. Stupid me. Why didn't I see that my baby girl was already sexually active? Her dad and me were in denial. Anyway, this particular Friday, I said to Wayne, "Don't go to work today as I want to take a water sample to the chemist." He said, "Why, what's wrong with you?" Gosh, how could I say, "I think our Nic is pregnant"? I didn't want to come out with it, but at the same time I couldn't lie. Well, when I told him, he replied, "She better not be!" That morning, I said to Nicola, "Can you do a wee sample, as I need to take it into the doctors to see if you have a water infection. Maybe that's why your periods are playing up." I really didn't want to say, "You could be pregnant." So, Nic went off to school and Wayne and I went to the chemist. My mind was stressing and my heart was racing. I didn't say a thing in the car; I just prayed we were wrong. So, in we went with the wee bottle and we waited and waited. Then I can remember a little Indian man coming out. He said, "Mr and Mrs Masters, congratulations – it's positive!" I burst into tears and said, "Oh fuck!" Thinking back now, the guy must have wondered why I was crying and swearing. I got into our car still crying and Wayne didn't say a thing. The day dragged and I can remember one of our neighbours, Sharon, knocking on our door. As soon as I saw her, I burst into tears again. "What's wrong, Mand," she asked. "It's our Nic, she's pregnant," I sobbed. Sharon was shocked too.

So, the time had come and our girl was due home. I was still crying and thinking back to the reading I'd had when Nic was 10. I said to Wayne, "You're gonna have to tell her." I was still so upset. Well, when she came in, I was looking out the lounge window with tears rolling down my face. I heard her dad say, "Sit down," and then he showed her the confirmation note. "What's this?" Nicola asked. "You know what it says," Wayne replied. "Pregnant." Nic started to cry and I said that we needed to go and tell the boyfriend's mum. Nic was just so worried that Wayne was going to hit him.

I had only ever seen the boyfriend, Kevin, a few times, and to be honest, I didn't think he was our daughter's type. We met his mum, Rose, and we were all in total shock. Wayne didn't believe in abortions, but he sat with our Nic and asked her what she wanted to do. She said that she wanted to keep her baby. "You will have to look after the baby yourself," I told her, "and keep on at school." Nic attended classes until she started to show and then we were told about a school where pregnant girls could go before and after having their baby. And bless her, that's what Nicola did. I was actually getting quite excited about becoming a grandparent. I was going to be called 'Nanny' – wow. As Nicola's due date neared, I went to see my own mum.

I was worried about being at the birth alongside Kevin. I was a little upset that I wasn't going to be able to hold Nic's hand or cuddle her, as a way to reassure her that everything was going to be OK. I felt a little angry that I had no arms. People often asked me, "Do you miss your arms, Mandy?" I would reply, "No, because I've never had them to miss." My dear mum could see I was getting upset and she said, "Mandy, ask the hospital if I could be with you, too." The rule was that only two people could be in attendance, but Mum said that if she were allowed in, she would be my arms and hold Nic for me. Oh, I'm welling up just typing this. I felt so relieved and Mum gave me a big cuddle. Thanks Mum – that meant so much to me.

The day arrived. Nic went into labour on the 28th August 1997. Me, my mum and Kevin were in the birthing room while Kevin's family waited outside, along with Wayne and Marie. My dear daughter was in so much pain and crying. I was so pleased that my dear mum was there with me. Kevin looked so worried too. Nicola had a very long labour, bless her, and then I witnessed the most beautiful thing. I could see what looked like a little wrinkled walnut coming out and then, OMG, out popped our little grandson, Callum Lee Michael. We were all crying, and then everyone else came in. Wow, I was a nanny, Wayne was a granddad and Marie was an auntie. My dear mum was now a great-grandmother. Phew, what a long day, but my God was it worth it. Boom – I'd finally got my cherry on the cake. Kevin became our son-in-law and he grew on me. Seeing my daughter happy and in love made Wayne and I happy, too. Yep, the cherry was gleaming and my cake was finished. I've conquered everything that those bloody negative doctors told my parents I wouldn't be able to do. Wow, what a journey. In no way was I going to be a cabbage. I've done it and I'm one happy nanny.

Conclusion

Well, what a journey I've been on, from learning to use my feet in everyday life, to growing up, putting up with all the stares and proving I can do things. I've dealt with some bad emotional stuff yet still picked myself up and carried on going forward. I've proved that I can lead a normal life and be around normal people. Stuff the people who never expected me to do all this – it's their loss not mine. I've never given up, as I know I was born different and that I'm here for a purpose. I also knew from an early age that I was spiritually connected, as the voice always spoke to me and reassured me that I was going to be OK.

I can now see why the spiritual side of me was lingering. It was preparing me for a special job and a very special journey. Many of you reading my story and learning about my childhood will know me as a walking earth angel. Yep, many people now know me as Mandy Masters, and not the girl with no arms. I won't tell you loads about my next journey, as I want you to read about that in Book Two, *The Earth Angel's Journey*. Believe me, the gift that was chosen for me from above is amazing. I've been given a spiritual gift and can connect to the above and beyond. I'm a well-known spirit communicator or medium, as you might say, but I really don't like that label, guys – I'm just an Essex girl with a difference. I was invited to join a well-known monthly magazine called *Take a Break Fate & Fortune* in 2005, and I'm still going strong now and contribute three pages.

Want to find out what totally changed me as a person (in a good way)? Well, watch this space. Goodbye Mandy Hornsby and hello Mandy Masters.

Thank you all for reading my book, *Mandy*, and I hope it opened your eyes as I went from a normal little girl, teenager and rebel, lol, to a married woman, a mum of two beautiful daughters and a grandmother of eight. After Nicola and Kevin had Callum, Dylan, Danny and little Kev came along. Then there are Tayler, Bailey, Ricky Roo and our bubs, Shay, who belong to Marie and her husband Ricky. Eight gawjuss grandsons – what more could I ask for? Ummm, well maybe some granddaughters – oh, yes please! I guess my family will grow and one day they will look proudly back and say to their families, "That's my Nan!"

Until next time...

About the Author

Mandy was born on the 20th September 1961. She was born Thalidomide, which means she was born without arms. At her birth there were three brothers and one sister, then another sister was born after Mandy.

Her parents were given a very bleak future for Mandy and the doctors suggested that as Mandy's prospects were not great, (the term cabbage was used) she could go to a home. They also said she probably wouldn't survive past her 19th birthday, but Mandy has proved them wrong.

Mandy attributes her success to her fantastic parents for bringing her up as a normal little girl. Her mother recalled a moment of Mandy's life, when she was just six months when she was lying in a pram and after hearing rustling noises realised that Mandy was playing with newspaper which was lining the pram. Her mother quickly got a plastic roller (which she used for her hair) and placed it over Mandy's toe – from that day forward she encouraged her daughter to use her feet.

Mandy started steadily walking from about nine months old her balance being very good (completely the opposite to what the doctors predicted. Mandy's parents were determined to get her into a normal main stream school, which she loved.

From that day onward Mandy has lived a normal life, she has just adapted her feet to do everything arms would. She was determined to live a full and varied life (which she certainly has) and is now married with two children and eight grandchildren. She works as a columnist at *Fate & Fortune* Magazine and as a spiritual connector to the above.

Mandy is a true survivor of Thalidomide.

Acknowledgements

First my husband, Wayne Masters, for not just being my hubby but my lover, best friend and soul mate.

My two beautiful daughters, Nicola Robinson and Marie Girling for being there for me and giving me and Wayne eight beautiful grandsons between them. The Robinson family, Son-in-law Kevin, grandsons Callum, Dylan, Danny and our little Kev and then the Girling family; Son-in-law Ricky, grandsons Tayler, Bailey, Ricky-Roo and our (Bubs) Shay. My family is my life, my achievements to show I've conquered Thalidomide. Who knows, I may even get a granddaughter OR great granddaughter, we will see!

My siblings Bill, Rob, Sue, Kev and Jane for putting up with me and my father Len. Donna Netting for always being there for me and Sandra and Margaret Archer who are my adopted family. Shirley Sibley (nee Hammond) for being by my side from five years old at school.

These are the ones I love that are now in Heaven; My dear Mum (Mumsi) my rock, my life my everything.

My sister Sue Jenner who passed too soon. Love you Sue.

My young handsome Nephew, Lee Hornsby missed so much.

A very, very dear adopted grandpa in Cornwall Tom Altree who was a special Medium/healer.

Waynes parents, my in-laws, Barbara and Lofty Masters.

My dear and bestie Julie Archer.

My beautiful cousin, Kenny Hornsby who I adored.

Aunt Joan and Uncle Fred, loved them dearly.

And to all my loved ones in Heaven, THANK YOU. XXX.